Church Flowers
Month by Month
Jean Taylor

D1111775

MOWBRAY
LONDON & OXFORD

First published in 1979 by A. R. Mowbray & Co. Ltd.,
Saint Thomas House, Becket Street,
Oxford, OX1 15J

Reprinted 1984

PRINTED IN GREAT BRITAIN BY
THE THETFORD PRESS LIMITED, THETFORD, NORFOLK

CONTENTS

INTRODUCTION

Church flower arrangers are dedicated people. Every week throughout the year they arrange flowers with loving care to make a more beautiful setting for the acts of worship and to remind us of the wonders of the world created by God.

This book has been written to assist them with ideas, reminders and references. There are suggestions for churches with limited, average and good resources, for city and country churches, for special occasions and major festivals and the both experienced and inexperienced flower arrangers.

Weather conditions and supplies of plant material vary considerably in different localities; therefore the average has been taken as a basis. But it is advisable to refer also to the chapters preceding and following each month. Many of the ideas are suitable for times other than the month in which they are shown. 'Flowers of the field' are included but only for areas in which they are plentiful in view of the need for conservation. Suggestions are made for some Saint days and books are listed which can provide further information for significant flower arrangements.

'. . . the experience of faith and the experience of beauty are in some measure identical' Van Ogden Vogt

A church calendar of English flowers

The Snowdrop in purest white arraie
First rears her hedde on Candlemass daie:
While Crocus hastens to the shrine
Of Primrose lone on S. Valentine.
Then comes the Daffodil beside
Our Ladye's Smock at our Ladye's tide;
Aboute S. George, when blue is worn,
The blue Harebells the field adorn.
Against the daie of the Holie Cross,
The Crowfoot gilds the flowrie grass.
When S. Barnabie bright smiles night and daie,
Poor Ragged Robin blooms in the haye.
The scarlet Lychnis, the garden's pride,
Flames at S. John the Baptist's tide;
From Visitation to S. Swithin's flowers,
The Lillie white reigns queen of the flowers,
And Poppies a sanguine mantle spread,
For the blood of the dragon S. Margaret shed.
Then under the wanton Rose again,
That blushes for penitent Magdalen,
Till Lammas Daie, called August's Wheel,
When the long Corn smells of Cammomile.
When Marie left us here belowe,
The Virgin's Bower is full in blowe;
And yet anon the full Sunflower blew,
And became a star for S. Bartholomew.
The Passion-flower long has blowed,
To betoken us signs of the holie rood:
The Michaelmas Dasie among dede weeds,
Bloom for S. Michael's valorous deeds,
And seems the last of the flowers that stood,
Till the feste of S. Simon and S. Jude,
Save Mushrooms and the Fungus race
That grow till All Hallowtide takes place,
Soon the evergreen Laurel alone is greene,
When Catherine crowns all learned menne;
Then Ivy and Holly berries are seen,
And Yule clog and wassail come round agen.

ANONYMOUS

JANUARY

This is a difficult month for flowers because they are scarce, expensive to buy and almost non-existent in the garden. There is a feeling of anti-climax and a need for economy after Christmas and there are weeks of cold weather ahead before the spring brings more garden flowers. Nevertheless at this time of the year flowers are often more appreciated than when they are plentiful and the church flower arranger will be certain of the congregation's enjoyment and admiration.

Surprisingly flower arrangers often do their best work at this time. Good design can come more easily when flowers are scarce and selection is not difficult. It is easier to concentrate on the design when there is less to choose from.

PLANT MATERIAL

The flowers that grow in the garden in January are usually small, such as winter jasmine, witch-hazel and early snowdrops, none of which are large enough for a church arrangement which can be seen by everyone. Nor do winter flowers last well indoors because they are used to a cold damp garden and a warm dry atmosphere does not suit them.

Shop flowers, though beautiful, are expensive because of the heat needed to grow them. It is therefore essential to find ways of stretching a few flowers into a big arrangement by adding other plant material from the countryside, a garden, or a stock of preserved and dried leaves and flowers. There are also several successful alternatives to flowers and no-one need feel that it is necessary to spend a lot of money. Simple evergreens, for example, can be just as lovely to look at when well arranged and they are an equally meaningful reminder of the beauty of nature.

Evergreens

Far more use could be made of evergreens. They are easy to find in gardens and countryside and they last well in water. Their green colouring is especially harmonious with stone and wood walls and reminiscent of early times when greenery was bound into garlands and stems were

7

strewn on the floors of churches. Now with modern mechanics and knowledge very big arrangements such as large pedestals can be made of evergreens alone.

Choice

It is more interesting to look at a number of greens in one arrangement. If you look carefully you can find yellow-greens, blue-greens, grey-greens, greens with variegation, plain and patterned greens, dark and

LIMITED RESOURCES *Evergreens in an economical arrangement for January. Arranger Jean Taylor. Photographer D. Rendell.*

Lilies, carnations, gladioli, irises and chrysanthemums arranged against a background of dark green, glossy camellia foliage for the memorial service in Westminster Abbey for Lady Churchill. By courtesy of The Flower Arranger. Arrangement by members of NAFAS.

light, shiny and dull greens and some greens are backed with another colour such as red or grey. Variety gives life to an arrangement, but the use of only one green can be monotonous.

Brighter greens, especially yellow-green, look attractive when used to emphasize the centre of a design instead of big flowers. Very light greens placed next to dark greens give good contrast in an arrangement to be seen from a distance.

A variety of textures also provides interest. For example, the rough appearance of yew, cupressus or fir can be combined with the smoother-looking leaves of laurels or bergenias and the shiny leaves of camellias or Magnolia grandiflora.

A list of suitable evergreens is useful so that you can ask for their location in gardens and when ordering new trees and shrubs for planting, but names are hard to remember and not necessary when you are looking for evergreens for an arrangement. Most of them last very well in water and are no problem, so cut different kinds, looking for contrasts in colour and texture. This will give an interesting group for arranging in a container.

Cutting

It is sensible to cut sparingly and only what you need because many evergreens take a long time to grow. A few long branches can be more effective than many short ones. Try to think of the arrangement as you cut. You will need plain, flat or dense leaves with short stems to conceal the mechanics; long branches for height and width; brighter greens for emphasis in the centre, and some contrasting textures. Look at the shape of a branch before cutting to make sure that it is suitable and preferably cut close to another branch or shoot to give it light and space to grow on. Cutting near a new shoot encourages it to grow well. Secateurs or a small sharp knife (if you can handle one) are better to use than flower scissors which may not be strong enough to make a clean cut.

Treatment

Although evergreens last well when cut and placed in water, some initial preparation is helpful. Many shrubs have hard, woody stems which protect them through the winter and prevent them from losing moisture, but the bark also prevents water from getting through from the outside, so it is a good idea to remove some of it. Using a small knife scrape off about 2-4 inches (5-10 cms). It is also helpful to slit up the end of a hard stem for about 2 inches (5 cms) to help the intake of water. Some people hammer woody stem ends but this is not necessary and the stems become more difficult to impale on a pin holder.

Some evergreens may be dirty and at this stage it is a good idea to swish them in a bowl of tepid water containing detergent. Stubborn dirt should be wiped off with a cloth. Damaged leaves should be cut away so that the final arrangement looks well-groomed.

Some arrangers like to submerge evergreens completely in a bath of water so that they become really full of moisture. However, although this is necessary for other foliage, it is not essential for evergreens and they can be arranged at once or stood in a bucket of tepid water until needed. If they are to be stored for any length of time before being arranged it is advisable to pull a large polythene bag over the top of the branches and the sides of the bucket to conserve moisture, especially with branches of fir which can drop its needles quickly.

*A polythene
bag conserves
moisture*

In the city

When evergreens are not obtainable from gardens or countryside, you may find that florists stock a selection including eucalyptus which is a lovely blue-green, pittosporum, camellia, cupressus, mahonia, box, laurel and the invaluable Western hemlock.

Evergreens for planting or locating

Branches

Blue Cedar	Rhododendron	Camellia
Pine	Spotted Laurel	Elaeagnus
Western Hemlock	Garrya elliptica	Golden Privet
Blue spruce	Cotoneaster	Holly

| Magnolia grandiflora | Eucalyptus | Sweet Bay |
| Deodar Cedar | Juniper | Picea pungens 'Moerheimii' |

Leaves to conceal mechanics

Skimmia	Magnolia grandiflora	Yew
Fatsia japonica	Choisya ternata	Euonymus
Laurel	Arum italicum	Box
Spotted Laural	Sweet Bay	Thuja

Yellow-green

Golden Privet	Elaeagnus pungens 'Maculata'
Euonymus	Elaeagnus x 'Limelight'
Skimmia	Golden Box

Holly, Ilex x altaclarensis 'Golden King' and Ilex aquifolium 'Golden Queen'

Chamaecyparis lawsoniana 'Lutea' and c. lawsoniana 'Lanei'

Cupressus macrocarpa 'Goldcrest'

Thuja occidentalis 'Rheingold'

Trails	*Interesting shape*
Ivy	Fatsia japonica
Japanese Honeysuckle	Mahonia x 'Charity'
Vinca	Spotted Laurel

Adding a few flowers

If you feel the need for flowers in addition to foliage, they can easily be placed in the centre of an arrangement of leaves. Start by arranging the foliage, saving the flowers until the end. Often the leaves will last for weeks and only a change of flowers will be necessary.

When only a few flowers are used in a design it is better not to scatter them about but to place them in a group in the centre or in an irregular line, where they will make more impact. A little space should be left around each flower so that the shapes can be seen clearly and they do not blur into a mass.

Three or five large flowers such as chrysanthemum blooms are sufficient, but there is no rule about using an uneven number. With smaller flowers such as daffodils and tulips a bunch of ten may be necessary. Spray chrysanthemums are usually available and if there are many flowers to a stem, three may be enough.

Preserved foliage

Foliage that has been preserved with glycerine during the summer months comes into its own in the winter. It can be an excellent substitute for fresh foliage, especially in city churches, and lasts indefinitely.

Preserved foliage is normally a shade of brown but in the same way that various greens look effective together, a variety of browns is more interesting than the use of only one brown in an arrangement. There are dark, almost black, browns and others range through tan and beige to cream. These shades harmonise successfully with yellow, orange and flame flowers and can be surprisingly attractive with white.

An arrangement of preserved foliage may seem lifeless to some people, but alters with the addition of a few flowers or some fresh green leaves or both. The fresh plant material can be placed in water as usual because the preserved foliage will come to no harm as long as it is dried between use. However, to prevent mould some arrangers dip the stem ends in varnish or bind them tightly with thin polythene before placing them in water.

Branches

Winter branches without leaves can look very striking and they are beautiful in a different way from flowers. When cutting them look for those with an interesting shape. Light walls will show them up well but if the church walls are dark try spraying the branches with matt, white paint or brushing them with emulsion paint. They combine well with white or cream flowers and a few leaves.

Branches of larch cones are much admired and these can be arranged with evergreens, preserved foliage and a few flowers. Good branches are blackthorn (but mind your fingers), Corylus contorta (Harry Lauder's Walking Stick) with lovely twists, Salix sachalinensis 'Sekka', a willow with twisted and flattened stems if pruned hard, Salix matsudana 'Tortuosa'. another willow with lovely curves, Rubus cockburnianus (Whitewashed Bramble) with a white waxy covering on the stems, a maple called Acer palmatum 'Senkaki'. But you will see other branches when looking around at winter trees and shrubs.

AVERAGE RESOURCES *Whitened winter branches with two stems of spray chrysanthemums and red cotoneaster berries in a grey and white stoneware container. Arranger Jean Taylor. Photographer D. Rendell.*

Spring bulbs

If bowls of bulbs were planted during autumn for use in the church they should be starting to show colour. If they are in clay or plastic plant pots these can be put in outer, more decorative containers.

Nurserymen, garden centres and florists often stock bowls of spring bulbs. These can be a better buy than cut flowers because they last longer, especially if bought when just showing colour. After the flowers have faded the bulbs can be planted in the church garden. Take the bowl out of the church, keep the bulbs watered and in March or April empty the bowl, compost, bulbs and all, and plant in the garden.

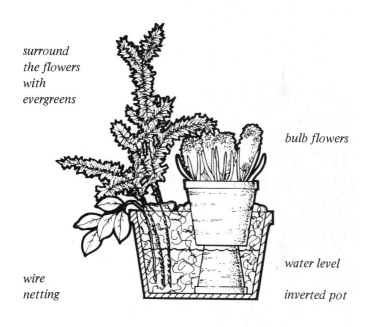

surround the flowers with evergreens

bulb flowers

wire netting

water level

inverted pot

If a bigger arrangement is needed a small bowl of bulbs can be placed in the centre of an arrangement of branches or evergreens in a large outer container. First upturn an empty plant pot, on which to stand the bulb bowl, inside the large container. Then the flowers will be seen clearly above the rim. Crumple wire netting, or add Oasis, inside the large container and around the back and sides of the pot to hold the stems of the fresh plant material. Water can be poured in for the stem ends, but it is better to avoid flooding the bulbs by keeping it below the bulb bowl.

Berries

The birds leave few berries for picking in January but there may be some snowberries which hang on for many months. Most are white but there are pink and pink-tinged varieties. These add interest to an arrangement of branches and flowers. The red berries of cotoneasters are often left by the birds and these add colour to a winter arrangement.

Catkins

It is early for most catkins but Garrya elliptica grows in some gardens. This has long, pendulous, grey-green catkins in January. They look their best when arranged so that the catkins hang downwards uncluttered by other plant material. Hazel or Cob-nut (Corylus avellana), a native shrub with yellow-green catkins, can be found in the countryside from January to March.

Fruit

It may seem strange at first to see oranges, lemons and apples in a January arrangement, because fruit is normally associated with harvest festivals. However, it can add colour to a winter arrangement, costs less than flowers and lasts well. If used sparingly it will not give the impression of autumn.

The circular shape of fruit makes it suitable for using in the centre of a design as a substitute for round flowers. It can also be used combined with flowers.

Impale the fruit on to a wooden skewer or a length of dowel-rod from a DIY shop. Push the other end into the mechanics of the arrangement, slanting the stick so that the fruit will not fall off it.

Ornamental cabbages

If these were sown during the previous year the coloured leaves can now be used in winter arrangements. Alternatively the whole plant can be pulled up and used as a rosette to hide mechanics or provide emphasis in a design of evergreens or branches. If the root is left on the plant, it can be replanted after the arrangement has passed its best. There are white or pink, plain or fringed leaf varieties, or 'Sekito' which is bright green and red.

Weathered wood

Many flower arrangers have a stock of weathered wood collected from lakesides, beaches and mountains and they may be willing to lend a few pieces to the church for January. Dramatic tall branches look especially effective in a modern or a country church combined with leaves and two or three flowers.

Treatment
It is unusual to pick up wood that is perfectly clean and most pieces need scrubbing in water containing detergent. Dry the wood and then brush with a wire hearth brush to remove dust, soft and loose wood. But be careful about scrubbing and brushing grey wood if you wish to keep the colour, since the greyness is only on the surface and can easily be removed.

Mechanics
Great care should be taken to make sure the wood is stable in the container. Light pieces of wood can be inserted into wire netting in a deep

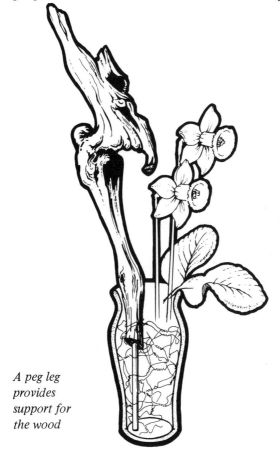

A peg leg provides support for the wood

container. Thinner stems can be impaled on a pinholder. Heavier and thicker stems need more preparation for stability.

A peg leg may be added to give support (with the permission of the owner of the wood). This leg can be made of dowel-rod. Another very firm support is plaster of Paris, obtainable in bags from a chemist. Fill a plastic plant pot with the powder and gradually stir in cold water. Insert the end of the wood into the plaster as soon as it is the thickness of whipped cream. Hold the wood firmly in position for a few minutes as the plaster sets. It is then easy to place the plastic pot in an outer, more decorative container and to use foam to support a few flowers and leaves near the wood.

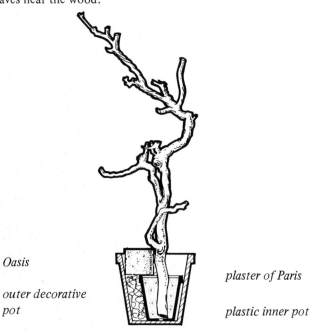

Oasis

outer decorative pot

plaster of Paris

plastic inner pot

Altar flowers

Most people prefer fresh flowers to be placed on the altar, although a grouping of evergreens can be very pleasing. The spring flowers such as narcissi, daffodils, irises, arums (see 'March' for hints on arranging) and early tulips are available in florists. A bunch of ten flowers should be enough for two altar vases if foliage is used. Not only does the latter stretch the flowers, but it softens the hard appearance of the rim of the container. Carnations, single chrysanthemums and roses are always available and are the right size for altar vases in the same way as spring flowers.

Foliage of laurel, smaller bergenias, Aucuba japonica 'Maculata' (Spotted Laurel), the mahonias especially Mahonia x, 'Charity', Elaeagnus pungens 'Maculata', E. pungens and Golden Privet are all available and the right size. Leaves variegated with yellow go well with brass altar vases and with white and cream flowers.

The stems of tulips have a tendency to change position after they are arranged, which makes them difficult flowers for altar vases. Blue

FOR THE ALTAR *Simplicity is often the most effective. Arum lilies from a florist with evergreen bergenia leaves from a garden arranged on a pinholder in a soft green container. Arranger Jean Taylor. Photographer D. Rendell.*

irises recede and cannot normally be seen from a distance. However, yellow and white irises, all the daffodils and narcissi and white lilies, which are usually in the shops, though more expensive than other spring flowers, can be used. Chrysanthemum blooms are usually available but tend to be associated with autumn, although the single chrysanthemums which look like daisies, such as white and yellow 'Bonnie Jean', seem to suit every season.

LIMITED RESOURCES

LIMITED RESOURCES, COUNTRY *Colourful dried flowers in mauve, yellow, pink arranged in a hidden container in St Martin's Church, Talke-o-the-Hill.*

LIMITED RESOURCES, CITY *Everlasting brown coconut palm spathes with two rosettes of long-lasting bronze-green Echeveria metallica in a brown stoneware container. Arranger Molly Duerr. Photographer D. Rendell.*

COUNTRY Some people do not like dried flowers in church because they feel it is the transient beauty and short life of fresh flowers that make them so precious and which interprets a philosophy of life which is meaningful in church. However, when resources are limited, dried flowers do add colour, and can be used as a second arrangement in another part of the church when the available money is spent on fresh flowers for the altar.

Nowadays arrangers have become skilful at drying flowers and keeping their colours. Pinks, blues, yellows and violets are retained well and from a distance can look like fresh flowers. There are many that can be dried successfully and a stock can be gathered during late summer for the church. (See page 169).

CITY A semi-permanent arrangement is economical and the leaves of houseplants or succulents can be used with driftwood or other natural plant material to last a long time.

Tall coconut palm spathes can be bought at florists and are everlasting. Rosettes of Echeveria metallica are bronze-pink in colour and look like flowers because of their shape. They can be used for emphasis in a design combined with preserved leaves and driftwood. Echeverias need little or no water and will last for a long time without attention and the cut stem ends can be impaled easily on a pinholder. When taken out of the container they will soon root again in compost. When handling be careful not to let the outer leaves break off. It is better also to avoid splashing water on the leaves because the waxy coating is easily marked. Simple stoneware containers suit the bold shapes.

IDEA OF THE MONTH

A simple cross can be made on two garden canes tied together at right angles using string or wire. The basic structure can be covered with dried and glycerined plant material in browns. Preserved cycas leaves (which look like palm) can be wired in two places to the canes to form a background. Then place a round of dry floral foam at the intersection of the canes and cover this with a cap of one-inch (2 cm) mesh wire netting. Secure this with two lengths of reel wire twisted on to the netting and carried round the back of the canes to be secured again on the other side of the netting. Dried and preserved plant material such as lotus seed pods (from a florist), preserved laurel leaves, dried poppy seed heads and trimmed palm can then be arranged in the foam. If you like a touch of gold paint, spray a light dusting on to the plant material.

IDEA OF THE MONTH *A simple cross of preserved cycas and laurel leaves with dried poppy seed heads, lotus pods and palm leaves. Arranger Peggy Crooks. Photographer D. Rendell.*

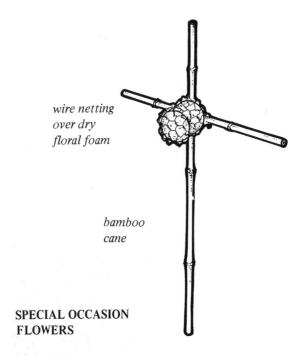

*wire netting
over dry
floral foam*

*bamboo
cane*

SPECIAL OCCASION
FLOWERS

Wedding flowers
(see February for other occasions) Pedestal arrangements of flowers can be very expensive for a January wedding and few families wish to go to the expense. Beautiful fresh spring flowers such as narcissi and Lilium longiflorum on the altar may suffice.

A more festive atmosphere is given if small posies can be secured to the front pews. These are easy to make. Wrap a round of soaked Oasis in thin polythene and then in one-inch (2 cm) mesh wire-netting. Twist a long length of reel wire or decorative cord to either side of the netting to attach the posy to the pew end. Starting with foliage first to make the most of the flowers make an arrangement in the Oasis. If necessary use a skewer to make holes for the softer flower stems, to stop them from breaking when they are pushed in. Avoid making holes in the underside of the polythene parcel because water will drip out. Some curved stems of ivy and a length of ribbon can add trails. Wind a short length of reel wire or a stub wire around the centre of a metre of ribbon and push the wire into the Oasis to hold the ribbon in place.

When larger arrangements are wanted evergreens will stretch the flowers, but the daintier varieties are more in keeping with a wedding. Western Hemlock is available from florists and is very pretty with long graceful branches. It can be cut in the countryside sometimes. Placed

AVERAGE RESOURCES *A simple and economical design of yellow roses with foliage for pew ends and to set the atmosphere for a wedding. Arranger Winifred Frame. Photographer D. Rendell.*

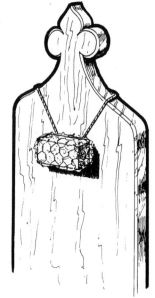

decorative cord or thin wire

wire netting over a polythene parcel of Oasis

in a polythene bag in a cool place it lasts for weeks and can be purchased well in advance of the occasion. The leaves are green on one side and grey on the other and both sides can be used in the arrangements to give a sense of lightness. A few plain leaves such as those of light green Skimmia japonica, rhododendrons or bergenias can be used to cover the mechanics. Then add a few stems of white Lilium longiflorum. If more flowers are wanted include carnations or single spray chrysanthemums, in white or yellow, either side of the lilies. Other spring flowers have stems, which are too short for a large arrangement but they can be used if placed in cones to give them height.

When flame colouring is asked for, Amaryllis can often be obtained. The stem is hollow but a length of dowel-rod can be inserted for placing into the mechanics. Make sure the end of the flower is in water or Oasis. Clivia has orange flowers but short stems. These can be arranged in several cones to give height. (See page 45).

FLOWERS AND FOLIAGE FOR FESTIVALS AND SAINT DAYS

January 1, New Year's Day

New Year's Day has been celebrated in Britain for the greater part of its history. It was one of the customs brought to Britain by the Romans who greeted each other with 'Happy New Year'. The wealthier citizens of ancient Rome used to give each other baskets of dates and figs.

Although Christmas is the more important occasion in most of England, people further north place more emphasis on welcoming in the new year.

The church celebrates on January 1 the circumcision of Jesus and His formal acceptance into the Jewish community. The eight sides of many church fonts are a reminder of the eight days between the birth of Jesus and the circumcision. A posy of flowers on, or near, the font would be appropriate.

John Wesley inaugurated the Watch Night Service which is held in many churches on the eve of the new year, a time for thinking about the past year and of making new resolutions for the coming year. The evergreens used in the church for Christmas should still be fresh for New Year's Eve and Day. The addition of a few young, spring flowers could make the arrangements significant of the old and the new years.

In Scotland New Year is called Hogmanay and it is thought the most likely origin of the word is the old French 'Au gui L'an neug' — 'To the mistletoe the new year'. According to Cotgrove (1611) this was the Druidical greeting given by revellers as they carried bunches of mistletoe from the woods. It would be symbolic of an ancient custom to include mistletoe in present-day church decoration at this time of the year.

January 6, Epiphany, Twelfth Night

Epiphany celebrates for the Christian the showing of Christ to people other than the Jews. The three 'Magi' or wise men presented their own significant gifts of gold for a king, frankincense for a great high priest, and myrrh for someone who would sacrifice his own life for the world. These traditional gifts are still ceremoniously presented at the altar in the Chapel Royal at St James Palace in London.

Christmas decorations are usually taken down on Twelfth Night, but if a crib is displayed in a church the figures of the three wise men should be added at this time. Other than decorations which especially belong to Christmas, there is no need to remove evergreens which, if still fresh, could remain with spring flowers added. Green or white is used significantly by some churches as the colour for the season of Epiphany.

FORWARD PLANNING

There is not much that can be done in gardens or countryside at this time of the year, although those people who grow lilies in pots in the greenhouse can now bring them indoors to force them for Easter. It is a good time to make up the church flower rota. There is also more time now to clean containers and mechanics, take stock and decide what is needed during the coming year, such as new containers, boxes of Oasis. Special mechanics, such as stands, could be made in readiness for the busy summer.

This can also be a time to gather together all the members of the congregation who volunteer to arrange the church flowers. A meeting could be held to discuss plans, new ideas and flowers for special occasions. Classes could be held for newcomers who would like to help – if they had more confidence in their own ability.

Lessons could include:
Mechanics and church containers, especially the use of altar vases. Scale and the use of larger flowers to be seen from a distance. Colour and its use in church for normal and for special services. The use of foliage to stretch flowers, the most long-lasting varieties, and how to condition leaves of various types. Conditioning flowers for long life.

The placement of flowers in the church in relation to existing church furnishings and the positions where flowers can be seen without obstructing the view or being in the way of people's movements. Methods of working which give the least amount of clearing up, such as the use of cardboard boxes and polythene or other sheeting. Sources of supplies such as gardens, nurseries and garden centres, markets and shops.

FEBRUARY

February is another cold, wintry month in Britain. Often there is snow and frost and the skies are heavy and grey. But in spite of the bare trees and the bleakness of the earth, there are signs of the spring soon to follow; tiny buds appear on branches and the shoots of bulb flowers begin to emerge through the hard ground.

PLANT MATERIAL

Florists' flowers
The spring flowers, daffodils, tulips, hyacinths, irises, clivias, polyanthus, freesias, anemones and lilacs are available, together with the usual all-season roses, chrysanthemums, lilies, carnations and imported gladioli. Dainty yellow mimosa arrives on the market but although lovely it soon dries up in a warm atmosphere. It can be used in a church arrangement (which is not expected to last all week) if it is kept in the polythene bag in which it is sold until the last minute before arranging. Spraying with a fine mist of water also helps to prolong its life.

Because spring flowers are becoming more plentiful and arriving from Cornwall, Devon and the Channel Islands in greater quantities, they should be less expensive than in January. These flowers can be used in small numbers combined with evergreens, bare branches, driftwood and glycerined foliage, in the same ways that are suggested for January.

Arranging bulb flowers
Bulb flowers of one kind or another are available almost all the year round, but the biggest choice is from just before Christmas to around Easter or even later in the north. Because they are available for so long, it is worth knowing about how to buy and condition them for a long life in flower arrangements.

Buying
If the flowers are to remain in the church all week then it is better to buy those with buds that are just beginning to show colour. In this case arrange them before Saturday so that they are open for the Sunday ser-

AVERAGE RESOURCES *Seven yellow gladioli, three white hyacinth, five yellow freesias and a few laurel leaves for lighting up a dark corner. Soaked Oasis to hold the flowers stands above the container's rim so that some plant material can be placed at an angle. This would be difficult with wire netting. The flowers, bought at the correct stage of maturity, will last well. Arranger Rona Coleman. By courtesy of the Bulb Information Desk.*

vices. If the flowers cannot be arranged until Saturday then it is preferable to buy flowers which are more mature so that there is more colour in the arrangements on Sunday. However, irises and daffodils often open overnight.

For long life buy anemones and freesias when they are only half open. Hyacinths should be hard and crisp with the top flowers tightly closed. Daffodils should be in the 'goose-neck' stage and tulips should be beginning to show colour; they are longer lasting than daffodils and irises. Only two or three gladioli flowers should be open on the lowest part of the stem because the buds open quickly, and once the top flowers are wide open and the lower ones are dead, the stem can look top-heavy in an arrangement. Lilies should have open only about a quarter of the total number of buds on the stem. They are often sold by the bud, so a single stem can be éxpensive if it has many buds. If possible buy lilies with one flower on a stem because these are easier to arrange.

Stems of bulb flowers should be stiff but if they are limp while still in tight bud they are in need of water. This can happen when the flowers have travelled some distance after cutting. They revive in an hour or two if the stem ends are placed in warm water. But when the flowers are well open and the stems are limp then the flowers are usually past their best and the stems are unlikely to stiffen up again.

Look for flowers with fresh green leaves, especially those of tulips which 'squeak' when fresh. The leaves of tulips can be placed separately from the flowers in an arrangement, but are easier to use if a small length of stem is left for impaling on the pinholder.

Conditioning

When you get the flowers home cut off about half an inch of the stem ends to remove any seal that formed while the flowers were out of water. Place the stems in a bucket or a jug containing 2 inches of tepid or warm water. Deeper water is not suitable for bulb flowers because the stem cell structure enables them to take up water easily and, as a result, they can become soggy with soaking and more difficult to arrange.

Young tulip stems are usually hard and crisp, but if they are at all limp wrap them firmly in newspaper before standing them in water for several hours to stiffen the stems. Despite this treatment tulips tend, of their own accord, to move in an arrangement and florists often wire them. But when used in an informal arrangement the movement does not matter.

Daffodils can exude a milky fluid which shortens the vase life of other flowers by clogging up stem ends and encouraging bacteria. Some flower arrangers condition them in a separate container before arranging them with other flowers. Others cut off the white part of the stem of daffodils because they believe this prevents the up-take of water.

Prolonging life

There are products sold by florists for lengthening the vase life of flowers. They contain a bactericide and can be added to the water in which flowers are placed; directions are given on the packets. The bactericide helps the cut ends of the stems to resist the attack of the harmful waste products produced by flowers and foliage as part of their natural metabolism. No food need be added to the water because there is adequate food already in the flower.

It is helpful to clean all containers before use with water containing bleach or disinfectant. The containers should be well rinsed. Dirty water, or water that has been used for other flowers, should never be left in the containers for new flowers. A stem is not selective in its absorption capacity and will take up any water, dirty or clean.

Use lukewarm water if possible, because this contains less oxygen which encourages the growth of bacteria around the stem end and thus shortens the life of a flower.

Remove the lower leaves from the stems because they deteriorate under water and produce harmful bacteria.

Spring flowers do not last as long as chrysanthemums and many summer flowers. They flower in cool weather in our gardens and their petal structure is unsuited to a hotter drier atmosphere, so their vase life is considerably shortened compared with their garden lives.

It is important that someone attends to arrangements of spring flowers in church after a few days if the arrangements are to remain there all week.

Mechanics

Most stems of bulbous flowers can be impaled easily on a pinholder or supported with wire netting. It is often said that they 'do not like' Oasis, but flowers will normally absorb water however it is supplied. Oasis is only unsuitable when a stem is soft rather than hard or crisp, because it will not go into it easily. This is often the case with mature daffodils. Hollow stems, such as those of amaryllis, cannot be pushed into Oasis easily and need a stick placed inside the stem like a splint. It should protrude for an inch or two, depending on the stem length. The stick can then be placed into the Oasis, but make sure the stem end reaches water. Hyacinths often have heavy heads, making them difficult to arrange. Thread a strong stub wire up each stem as far as the flower head. This gives support in an arrangement. It is a pity not to use hyacinths because they have a longer life than many spring flowers.

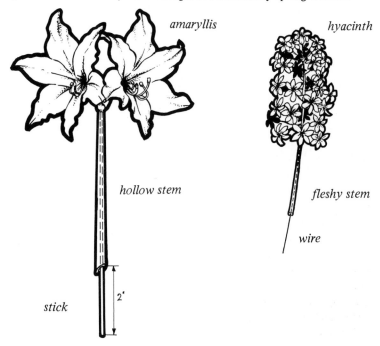

amaryllis   hyacinth

hollow stem   fleshy stem

wire

stick   2′

Garden plant material

Small flowers are still the only ones available in the garden, but a small grouping near the church entrance, where people coming in and going out may see it, can be very appealing. Sprigs of winter jasmine, witch-hazel if it is still available, heathers, snowdrops and Helleborus foeti-dus can be included. Hellebores flower in the garden during February, but the majority of them wilt in a few hours if cut at this stage. When the fruit develops later on they are suitable for cutting and last well. They are not seen easily from a distance, making them unsuitable for a major arrangement, and are better used nearer the entrance.

Evergreen foliage is freely available and at this time the perennial Arum italicum can be cut. The leaves are in good condition even when the plant is buried under snow, but the size of the leaves varies according to the part of the country in which the plant grows. Seed is a slow method of propagation and a clump obtained from a friend gives quicker results. The shape of the leaf makes it a useful cover for mechanics.

The hardy fern Polystichum setiferum 'Divisilobum' is very pretty and can often be cut at this time. It provides a change of shape from the smoother leaves of the bergenias, ivies and Arum italicum.

In most places it is too early to start forcing branches in a warm place indoors, although in milder parts of the country this may be possible.

LIMITED RESOURCES *Winter garden foliage including Arum italicum, periwinkle and skimmia are used to eke out three white or yellow chrysanthemum blooms and two stems of spray chrysanthemums, cut down. The large flowers placed at the centre are at differing angles and height. Arranger Madge Green.*

An economical but elegant arrangement of winter garden foliage in-cluding evergreen bergenias, hellebore leaves and ferns with dried sea hollies arranged in Oasis to achieve a gentle Hogarth curve in a green and gold container. Arranger Adele Gotobed. Photographer Peter A. **Harding. By courtesy of The Flower Arranger.**

Dried and fresh plant material

There is no reason why dried flowers should not be combined with fresh foliage to stretch resources at this time of the year. Fresh green bergenia leaves, the fern fronds of Polystichum setiferum 'Divisilobum', foliage of Arum italicum, elaeagnus, laurel, skimmia, rhododendron and bay can add life to an arrangement, with further colour supplied by the dried flowers such as the gold of yarrow, especially Achillea 'Gold Plate', the blues of sea hollies and delphiniums, the many oranges and reds of strawflowers (helichrysums), pinks and mauves of larkspur, and artichoke heads which can be dusted with gold spray paint.

Even if fresh flowers are preferred on, or near, the altar, dried flowers with fresh foliage can provide a second arrangement which saves the available money for buying florists' flowers.

Wild plant material

We are now conscious of the great need to conserve wild plants because of their rapid and often total disappearance; however, in countrysides where a plant grows in plenty it does no harm to cut sparingly. On the edge of the woods you can find hazel catkins (Lamb's Tails). Branches of these are excellent for providing height in an arrangement of spring flowers, few of which have long stems. The merry little catkins have great charm and show up quite well from a distance. There are also the brown catkins of the alder which grows in wet places during February and March, and the yellow catkins of the Balsam Poplar.

Sallow catkins (Goose-chicks) can be found in some places, and although they tend to look stiff they can give height in an arrangement.

Houseplants

Many modern churches have sufficient light for houseplants to be grown with success. It is essential to place the plants near a window. The winter sun will do them no harm, although in the summer months they should not be in direct, unfiltered light.

Plants add colour and natural, fresh beauty to a church in the same way as flowers, and because a church does not have extremes of cold or heat they should last well. February and March are good months to start them off because March to October is the growing period for pot plants.

A grouping of several plants in one bowl or trough is usually more effective than single plants scattered about, and plants usually thrive in a grouping because of the surrounding moist air. Choose a trough or a large, deep bowl such as a copper or brass urn, a jam pan, a Victorian wash-bowl, a garden urn or a modern pottery container made for plants. Chain stores sell inexpensive plastic copies of garden urns which can be painted stone colour with emulsion paint. Sand added to the paint gives a rough texture similar to stone and this blends in well with church walls.

Method

Place about 2 inches (5 cms) of gravel in the bottom of the bowl for drainage; gravel can be obtained from a builders' merchant and sometimes from garden centres. Sprinkle small pieces of charcoal on the top of the gravel to keep the water sweet. Then add a layer of John Innes No. 2 compost which is sold in bags. Charcoal and compost are available from garden centres. Knock out the plants from their pots and arrange them pleasingly on the compost. Add more compost, pushing it down well between the plants to bed them in, but leave a space of about 2 inches (5 cms) between the top of the soil and the rim of the container so that the plants can be watered without spillage. Also make sure that the top of the soil ball surrounding each plant is not covered with the new compost. If necessary lift up the plant by placing more compost underneath it.

compost
gravel

plants grow well in
a window trough

Choosing houseplants

When combining plants in one container it is important to plant together those which need the same conditions of light, temperature and moisture. For example, a hydrangea needs constant watering but a succulent needs little, and so only one or the other will survive. Go to a reliable garden centre or houseplant nursery for advice on plants for your church. It is advisable to buy those suitable for lower (but frost-free) temperatures because the heat is not turned on in a church all week. It is also advisable to buy plants labelled 'Easy to grow' because some need special temperatures or are difficult to grow without specialized knowledge or careful attention.

Shape, texture, colour

When combining plants the grouping is more attractive when plants with varying shapes and textures are used. Also if possible use more than one green, or a plant with variegated leaves, to add interest. Some plants which trail down over the rim of the container soften the appearance and ivies are excellent for this.

Flowering plants, though attractive for a while, are less permanent and not advisable for economy. Depending on the light and temperature of the church the following plants are easy to grow and survive in cooler air.

Aspidistra

Aucuba japonica
    (Spotted Laurel)

Bay trees

Begonia metallica

Camellia

Chlorophytum comosum
    (Spider Plant)

Cissus antartica
    (Kangaroo vine)

Fatshedera Lizei
    (Fat-headed Lizzie)

Fatsia japonica

Ficus elastica robusta
    (Rubber plant)

Grevillea robusta
    (Silk Oak)

Heptapleurum arboricola
    (Green Rays)

Ivies of all varieties

Monstera deliciosa
    (Swiss cheese plant)

Neanthe bella
    (Parlour Palm)

Peperomias

Pilea (Aluminium plant)

Poinsettias (for Christmas)

Rhoicissus rhomboidea
    (Grape Ivy)

Sansevieria trifasciata laurentii
    (Mother-in-law's Tongue)

Schefflera

Tradescantia
    (Wandering Sailor)

Hydroculture for easy work

The now popular method of growing plants in water, called hydroculture, is especially suitable for buildings where plants are left unattended for some time. Watering is only necessary every two or three weeks and an indicator shows when this is necessary. Feeding is only required every six months for larger plants and once a year for smaller ones. Garden centres and houseplant nurseries have plants for sale grown by this method and will recommend those suitable for a church. The cost may be high initially but the plants will last for months, probably years, and will be an economical buy in the long run.

ALTAR FLOWERS

Simple arrangements, perhaps of one type of flower with foliage, are usually appropriate for the altar or communion table. It may be the custom to use special altar vases but if not, a bowl which can hold a large pinholder is easy to arrange with spring flowers — especially for a flower arranger who is a beginner.

The container should not be conspicuous and should provide a background for the flowers rather than vie with them. The earthy colours,

FOR THE ALTAR *Daffodils and light green skimmia foliage arranged to show each flower clearly in a dark brown glass bowl. The central flowers face forwards and the others turn away to show the sides and backs of the flowers. Arranger Jean Taylor. Photographer D. Rendell.*

soft, subtle or dark, are the best, such as brown, beige, dark green, grey, grey-blue. White is not a good colour because, unless white plant material is used, it tends to separate from the flowers and attract too much attention from them.

First arrange a few leaves, such as skimmia, privet or elaeagnus. Spring flowers tend to be small in comparison to summer and autumn flowers so the leaves should be in scale with them. If you use the foliage of daffodils it is easier to tie a few leaves together with yarn before impaling them. The woody stems of most evergreens can easily be impaled on a pinholder.

Then add one or more bunches of flowers, leaving a little space around each flower so that its shape can be seen clearly. Turn the flowers to face in different directions, with those in the centre facing to the front and the others gradually turning away. Any placed at the back of the arrangement should face towards the rear. This gives depth and interest because the sides and backs of flowers, especially daffodils with their distinctive shape, are just as lovely as their faces.

Simplicity in flower arrangement can be most beautiful, so do not feel that you 'have not done enough'. The aim is to show the beauty of the flowers and to avoid hiding the permanent fabric and furnishings of the church.

LIMITED RESOURCES

Country

Baskets of all types seem suitable for a country church and for spring flowers. They do not hold water so it is necessary to use an Oasis saucer, a food tin painted with dark paint or a similar plastic container to hold water and mechanics. This container, which is utilitarian and not decorative, can be concealed with moss, stones, small pieces of driftwood or flat short-stemmed leaves such as those of Arum italicum, laurel, elaeagnus, skimmia or ivy.

*saucer
for mechanics*

Branches of hazel catkins from the countryside are good for height and can be impaled easily on a pinholder or pushed into soaked foam. They cannot be supported firmly by wire netting when it is used without a pinholder in a small container.

A bunch of five daffodils from a florist or sheltered garden may be

LIMITED RESOURCES, COUNTRY *Hedgerow hazel catkins and ivy leaves with a bunch each of florists' daffodils and tulips arranged in a saucer of foam concealed with moss, stones and bark on a wicker tray. Arranger Rona Coleman. By courtesy of the Bulb Information Desk.*

sufficient if foliage is also used. A grouping of five tulips (usually one bunch from the florist) can be added if resources permit. In a naturalistic style, using a basket container or base, it does not matter if, after several hours, the tulips change position of their own accord.

If no funds are available for flowers then a small grouping of garden flowers such as snowdrops or winter jasmine can be placed at the base of the design. In this case more hazel branches and transitional foliage such as Golden Privet may be necessary to fill in the middle part of the design. However, the catkins can be seen more clearly if some space is left around them.

This style of design is not only economical but it lasts well, because the background branches and foliage can remain for several weeks with a replacement of flowers only when necessary.

LIMITED RESOURCES, CITY
An arrangement of early narcissi with elaeagnus foliage; one of a pair of designs suitable for a modern altar or elsewhere. Arranger Madge Green.

The design is built up on a cone of wire netting.

City

Foliage is often hard to find in a city but a design can be made using two or three bunches of florists' daffodils, narcissi or tulips. A twig or two of foliage can be added if available. A tall stoneware container is more suitable for a modern church, but similar designs can be made in the traditional altar vases.

Crumple strong 2 inch (5 cms) mesh wire netting into a long thin cone shape and push it down to the bottom of the container. Pull the remainder well above the rim, almost to the height of the tallest stem. Cut the stems of the flowers to different heights and thread them through the wire netting and into the water, turning the flower heads gradually away from the centre.

IDEA OF THE MONTH

A bowl of houseplants in a church can be given colour with the addition of a few fresh flowers. The plants make a permanent decoration so that the church always has some green plant material, with or without flowers. But before the Sunday services or for special occasions, cut flowers can be added to the bowl of plants to provide extra colour. The plants may need replacement from time to time, but this makes a very economical permanent decoration, with endless variations. Remember, however, that the plants need light and the choice of plants is important (as previously described under 'Houseplants'). This style of design is called a *pot-et-fleur,* meaning pot plants and cut flowers.

A small bunch of flowers is all that is necessary. In spring, gladioli or lilies can give height or shorter-stemmed flowers can be placed lower down among the plants. Other seasonal flowers can be used later, such as peonies, poppies, marguerites, large roses in summer; dahlias, sunflowers and chrysanthemums in autumn; holly berries and poinsettias for Christmas.

A small container is necessary for the flowers. It is easier to push this into the compost in the centre front at the time of planting. An empty lidless food tin painted dark brown or black, big enough to hold water for the flowers, is suitable. A pinholder can be used, with or without wire netting, or Oasis can be placed in the container for supporting the flowers. The container will be concealed by the compost and the foliage of the plants.

SPECIAL OCCASION FLOWERS

Suggestions for wedding flowers are made under January and similar

IDEA OF THE MONTH *A pot-et-fleur in a brass container with grow-ing plants and cut stems of lilies and gladioli. The plants are ivies, peperomias and tall Mother-in-law's Tongue. These plants need soil that is left to dry between waterings but the ivies and peperomias should be sprayed sometimes. Arranger Margaret Muirhead. Photographer D. Rendell.*

styles are suitable for February.

Very often it is necessary to make large decorations for special occasions such as memorial services, festivals or other events. At this time of the year this is difficult unless resources and funds are

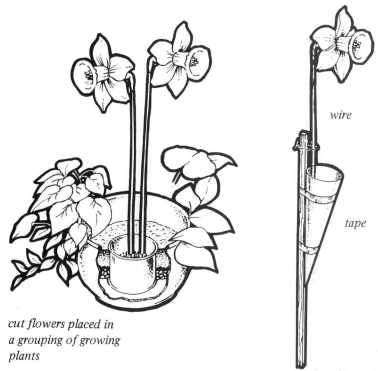

*cut flowers placed in
a grouping of growing
plants*

wire

tape

*a cone or tube of water
taped to a stick to
give height*

readily available. In this case plenty of flowers can be used, but it is still better to start with foliage, whether from a garden, market or shop, because this provides a good background to show up the flowers.

Flowers with long stems are hard to find, although gladioli and lilacs are available. Shorter-stemmed flowers can be placed in tubes or cones bound with sticky tape in two places to a long stick, to give height. The tubes can be filled with water and crumpled wire netting or with soaked Oasis. A square stick is easier to use than a round one because the tube does not slip as easily. It is better to paint the tube and the stick with a dark green or black matt paint so that it is unobtrusive. If the stick protrudes a few inches above the top of the tube, taller or unstable flowers can be wired to it for a second support.

It is important to conceal the tubes and sticks with foliage or flowers placed in front of them. For this reason use as few tubes as possible to provide height to the flowers in the design, which otherwise becomes cluttered and heavy in appearance.

SPECIAL OCCASION FLOWERS *White lilies, tulips, irises and daffodils with blue irises and hyacinths placed in cones to give height with rosemary, bay, Senecio cineraria maritima, Eucalyptus gunnii and juniper foliage, pussy willow and black poplar catkins in a 7 foot high arrangement for the memorial service for Lord Avon in Westminster Abbey. Arrangers Joan Weatherlake and Edna Johnson. Photographer James Fenemore. By courtesy of Amateur Gardening.*

A garland of foliage

If a person is especially to be remembered on a specific day, a garland of evergreens can surround a memorial stone. Plentiful foliage such as cupressus and laurel are advisable, because garlands take a surprising amount of plant material. Try to find contrasting shapes and textures and a variety of greens to give interest. Make sure the foliage is clean; it may need washing in warm water containing a detergent.

The easiest way of making a garland is to use a polythene tube filled with small blocks of soaked Oasis or with damp moss ordered and bought from a florist. Polythene tubing can be bought from mail order firms which advertise in gardening magazines. Alternatively buy thin polythene sold by the metre in hardware shops. Cut this into strips of about 4 inches (10 cms) in width, and any length. Machine (using the longest stitch) or hand sew the edges together to make a tube.

If the garland is to be straight, push the blocks of Oasis close to-gether. Moss, which is more economical, should be placed firmly into

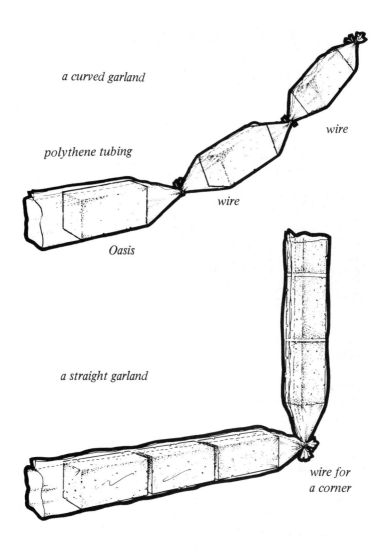

a curved garland

polythene tubing

wire

wire

Oasis

a straight garland

wire for a corner

the tubing. If it is to be curved then leave spaces between the Oasis blocks or the moss and tie these with wire or thread like a string of sausages. This enables the garland to be curved easily.

Push short woody stems straight through the polythene into the foam or moss. If stems are pushed in on a slant the mechanics are soon covered. Softer stems may not go easily through the polythene and it is better to make a hole with a sharp, pointed implement first. If a long garland is necessary it is quicker to use plant material with woody stems.

SPECIAL OCCASION FLOWERS *Evergreens, cupressus and laurel in a garland placed around the memorial stone to Sir Winston Churchill in Westminster Abbey on the occasion of Lady Churchill's memorial service. Arranger Mary Napper. Photographer Dennis Barnard. By courtesy of The Flower Arranger.*

Garlands of foliage last a long time, but also take time to make, so it is a good idea for two or three people to work together for quick progress in a congenial atmosphere.

Preserved, dried and fresh plant material

A large arrangement must often depend in the winter months on dried and preserved foliage and seedheads with, sometimes, the addition of a few fresh flowers.

Height can be obtained by lifting the arrangement on to a pedestal or covered stand. Height is so important if an arrangement is to be seen by everyone in the congregation. Long-stemmed Bells-of-Ireland (Molucella laevis) and Pampus Grass, both either dried or preserved in glycerine (see page 167), provide height and a light cream colour. Fresh evergreens and ferns, mixed with dried and preserved leaves in many browns from light to dark, make an interesting design with plenty of variety in the colour scheme of green, brown and cream.

If a brighter colour is desired then yellow or white single spray chrysanthemums, white lilies, lilacs or gladioli can be used. Wide open tulips are also lovely.

Two arrangements give more impact around a statue or memorial, but it is usually better to have them in unequal sizes, one smaller and one larger, and at different heights. They can be linked with trails of foliage and in some cases with unobtrusive fabric.

Dried, cream Bells-of-Ireland and Pampas Grass with garden foliage in Southwell Minster. Although a large display, it is economical. Arrangers from Heanor Flower Club. Photographers, Lead, Nutt and Stevens.

Plant materials for festivals and Saint days

2 February – Candlemas

Candlemas is the feast of the purification of the Virgin Mary (or the presentation of Christ in the temple). It is usually celebrated with many candles, the symbolism being the commemoration of the entry of the 'True Light' into the world. Snowdrops are sometimes called Candlemas Bells or February Fair Maids. Although too small for the main flower arrangement in the church, a small grouping on the altar or near to the entrance of the church can be both appealing and significant. They are unlikely to last more than a few days and may need renewing during the week. In seventeenth century England it was a country custom to take down the last greens of the old year.

14 February – St Valentine's Day

It is difficult to find out much about Valentine, a Saint whose festival is better known than his life, but it is thought that he was an Italian put to death for his faith some time during the third century in the reign of Emperor Claudius II. He fought against the un-Christian edicts of the emperor and for this he was beheaded. One of the edicts was that soldiers should not marry, but Valentine performed the marriage ceremony in secret. When he was put into jail it is said that he fell in love with the jailer's daughter and on the day he was led to his execcution he left a note addressed to her and signed 'Your Valentine'.

There are many traditions that refer to the choosing of sweethearts associated with St Valentine's Day, most of which are not suitable for interpretative arrangements in church. Also traditional heart shapes are not normally in keeping with the church building. It is enough to arrange young flowers in pretty colours to signify the first stirrings of spring.

FORWARD PLANNING

Amaryllis

The flowers of the many beautifully-coloured flowers of Amaryllis, also called Hippeastrum or Barbados Lily, are especially suitable for church decoration because of their size, bright colouring of red, flame, pink, white and orange, and lasting ability. Bulbs can be planted from February to April for flowering in late March to June.

Soak the roots and the lower part of the bulb in tepid water for about five days. Plant in a pot which gives about an inch of space all round the bulb and has crocks in the bottom, because good drainage is essential. Use John Innes No. 2 or 3 compost mounded into a cone and place the bulb on top with the roots spread out. Add more compost leaving about half the bulb above the soil after planting. Water and place in a position where the bottom of the plant can be warm, such as on a radiator shelf, a mantelpiece over a fire, the top of the television set or in an airing cupboard. After two weeks use tepid water sparingly on the compost (not the bulb) and make sure the temperature around the bulb does not drop below 60°. As soon as a bud appears move the pot to a sunny window and then as the flowers begin to show colour it can be used in the church.

The pot can be placed in a larger container surrounded by evergreens to make a big arrangement. It can remain without re-potting for 3-4 years. If the flower is cut for use in an arrangement try to cut off as little of the stem as possible. This should be left on the bulb until it has yellowed when it should be cut off close to the bulb. After flowering continue to water the bulb and leave it in the sun, but gradually reduce water from late August, keeping the bulb dry from the end of September in a cool room. After three months the growth cycle can be started again by watering and warmth.

Annual and biennial seeds
Seeds should be ordered at once for sowing in preparation for summer flowers. Useful for church arrangements and for drying and preserving are.

Helichrysum bracteatum (Straw Flower) which can be dried and used for several years in winter. The largest form is H. 'Tetraploid'. The flowers can be cut during July and September. Seeds can be sown outside in April or May, or in colder areas can be started under glass in February and March and hardened off before planting out in May.

Amaranthus caudatus (Love-lies-bleeding) has red or green tassel flowers from July to October which provide long trails for graceful arrangements. Sow seeds in March under glass to plant out in May or sow in flowering position in May, thinning out as necessary.

Nicotiana affinis (Tobacco Plant) 'Sensation Mixed' and 'Lime Green' are popular and provide tall, long-lasting small flowers in June-September which are good for filling in, although not big enough for emphasis flowers. Sow under glass in February or March for planting out in May.

Papaver somniferum (Opium Poppy) has white, red, pink or purple flowers up to 4 inches across in June and August. Sow in the flowering site in March and April, just covering them with soil. They often seed themselves. The seedheads will dry.

Phlox drummondii 'Grandiflora' with larger flowers from July-September are useful for summer arrangements. Sow seeds in pots or boxes during March under glass, plant out in May.

Zinnia elegans with colourful flowers including green 'Envy'. The rounded shape is excellent for focal points in arrangements. Sow the seeds under glass in March and plant out in May and June for flowering July-September.

Gaillardia aristata (Blanket Flower) with gay red, yellow and orange flowers in daisy shape from June to October. Seeds can be sown in the flowering site in April and thinned out, or sow under glass in February or March, planting out in May.

Antirrhinum (Snapdragon) The taller form, A. majus 'Maximum', is useful for church decoration with a height of 3–4 feet, flowering from July after sowing seeds under glass in February or March; plant out in May–June.

Angelica archangelica, a hardy biennial which will seed itself. The round green flowers in July and August grow on stems from 6-10 feet and are spectacular in an arrangement. Sow seeds in March or April out-of-doors.

Matthiola incana (Stock). The Ten Week stock is treated as an annual and is good for cutting. The double-column types have extra long stems with one dense flower to a stem. Sow seeds in February or March under glass and plant out in April or May, or sow directly in flowering site in April.

Molucella laevis (Bells-of-Ireland) provides long spikes which glycerine well for winter use. The seeds can be difficult to propagate but are well worth the trouble. Sow in March under glass in a temperature of $59°$, for planting out in May, but the really long spikes are normally produced entirely under glass.

Lunaria annua (Honesty) The form with white flowers is more useful for the church than the violet, but it is the silvery flat seed pods that are invaluable for winter use. This is a biennial which seeds itself. The leaves are most useful in winter. Sow new seeds in May or June in flowering position for flowers the following year.

Onopordon acanthium (Scotch Thistle) A hardy biennial which grows to a height of 6 feet and provides dramatic plant material for arrangements in July and August. Sow the seeds in May out-of-doors for next year or under glass in March for planting out in May.

Calendula officinalis (Pot Marigold) with brilliant orange and yellow shades which last well when cut and flower from May until the first frost. Sow in March for summer flowering or in September for late spring flowering. The more they are cut the more flowers are produced.

Delphinium consolida (Larkspur) is useful to grow because it can be dried for winter use. The blue, pink, mauve and white flowers can grow to a height of 4 feet. The Giant Imperial strain is good for cutting and the Stock-flowered group is the most popular, growing up to 3 feet high. Sow in flowering site in March or April.

Dianthus barbatus (Sweet William) grown as a biennial has small but brightly coloured flowers in June and July. For flowering the same year sow the seeds under glass in March and plant out in May.

Digitalis (Foxglove) is self-seeding but first seeds can be planted outside in May or June for flowering the following year, or under glass in February or March to flower the same year in July and August. The cut flowers are excellent to give height in a summer arrangement, but also the seedheads can be preserved with glycerine for winter use.

Helianthum annuus (Sunflower) is useful for really big yellow flowers July-September. Sow seeds in March or April in a sunny position out-of-doors, or in February under glass, planting out in May. 'Italian White' is a creamy colour.

Rudbeckia (Coneflower) Late summer flowers which last well; sow in March or April and plant out in May.

Verbascum bombyciferum (Mullein) is a biennial with useful grey leaves and yellow flower spikes in June and July from seeds sown in a cold frame in April and moved to next year's flowering site in September.

Cucurbita pepo (Ornamental Gourd) Gourds are useful for harvest festival decoration and for selling at bazaars. They can also be dried for winter decoration. The seeds should be soaked in warm water before planting in peat pots 6-8 weeks before the expected last frosts in your area. Plant out two weeks after the last expected frost.

Dipsacus fullonum (Fuller's Teasel) Useful prickly heads to dry for winter arrangements. Frost resistant but dies after flowering. Germination 1-2 weeks and easy to grow.

Details of cultivation are normally printed on the back of seed packets. It is important that seedlings are not planted out until the danger of frost has passed and this varies in different parts of the country.

Members of the church flower guild or group may like to share the growing of a number of annuals and biennials. The flowers, seedheads and leaves will eventually make an important economic contribution to the church flowers, apart from being enjoyable in the garden.

Gladioli

Order or buy gladioli corms for cut flowers during summer and autumn. Their size and colouring makes them ideal for use in church decoration.

MARCH

This month has very pronounced weather variations, both from day to day and from year to year. The contrast between the weather in the north and the south of Britain is at its greatest, so it is difficult to suggest flowers that can be used in churches all over the country. Spring may have started in parts of Cornwall but winter may be still bitterly cold in northern Scotland.

The flowers from the warmer south, however, become more plentiful and consequently less expensive in shops everywhere, and some flowers that can be used in church arrangements begin to appear in gardens.

Easter sometimes falls in this month as it can be any time between 22 March and 25 April. Suggestions for arrangements for the Easter season are made under both months.

PLANT MATERIAL

Florists' flowers

More plant material is available in March than in the previous two months and there are many varieties and colours of spring flowers from which to choose, in addition to the 'all-the-year-round' flowers. Prices may rise around Easter because of demand.

Strelitzias (Bird-of-Paradise Flowers) can be seen in some shops. These dramatic flowers, often imported, are very expensive but may last several weeks. The petals can be cut off as they fade and others eased from the bracts. The stems are long and strong and the flowers brilliant, which makes them ideal for church arrangements. Two or three may be sufficient for an arrangement when combined with foliage or other flowers. Members of the congregation travelling abroad may be able to purchase them at a much lower cost than at home.

Flowering pot plants

At this time of the year, when resources are limited, flowering pot plants can be a better buy than cut flowers because they last longer. They can be bought from florists and garden centres and can be combined with evergreens in one outer container in the same way as pots of bulbs (see page 15).

Azaleas
These last well in a cool position, especially if they are watered frequently and sprayed sometimes. Faded flowers can be picked off. If gradually acclimatized to outdoor conditions they can be planted in a garden once the danger of frosts is over.

Hydrangeas
Pots of hydrangeas are especially effective at this time of the year and will last a long time providing they are never allowed to dry out completely. They need much water and in a warm room daily watering is necessary. It is helpful to stand the pots in an outer decorative container which has a layer of wet peat or of gravel and water. If the plant wilts, plunge it immediately into a bucket of tepid water and it should revive in a few hours. Avoid standing pots in a sunny window or near a radiator. Hydrangeas can be planted out after frosts but need to be acclimatized gradually to outdoor temperatures.

Chrysanthemums
Chrysanthemum plants are available the whole year and the varieties with single flowers in yellow and white seem more suitable than others for spring. They have excellent keeping qualities and need regular but not copious watering. Unless you are expert at taking cuttings it is usual to discard the plant after flowering.

Cinerarias
The daisy-like flowers in many colours are very pretty. They need regular watering, but over-watering may cause the plants to collapse prematurely. They do not last long as azaleas, chrysanthemums or hydrangeas, but are less expensive to buy. They are normally discarded after flowering.

Cyclamens
Hot, dry rooms are unsuitable for cyclamens but in a cool church they may thrive. Excessive wetness or dryness should be avoided. Use tepid water and pour in on to the soil, not the plant, allowing it to dry out between waterings. This plant is often discarded after flowering.

Garden plant material
Although there is still little from which to choose in gardens some early

spring flowers are beginning to appear. Evergreens must still be used for foliage because deciduous foliage is either unobtainable or too young to use. Signs of spring show in buds growing on trees and shrubs, and in some cases these can be forced into bloom or leaf earlier than usual.

Camellias

Camellias are flowering at this time and some church members may have shrubs big enough to cut. The foliage is extremely long-lasting and beautiful and, even when the short-lived flowers fade or drop off the branches, the leaves can remain in an arrangement while other spring flowers are added. The foliage is often obtainable from florists.

Forcing flowers and leaves

Whatever the tree or shrub the guideline is to cut branches with large buds, because these are nearer to opening time and easier to force.

Scrape off 2 inches (5 cm) of the outside bark and split the stem end of the branch. Place it immediately in several inches of water that has just come to the boil. Leave this to cool and then fill up the container with tepid water. Stand it in a sunny window or a warm room. Soon

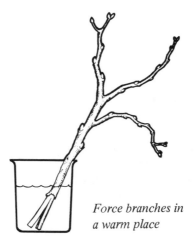

Force branches in a warm place

the buds should begin to open. If you are in a hurry for results, change the water frequently, substituting hot water each time.

It is fascinating to watch buds of flowers or leaves gradually unfurl. Bare branches can be placed in water in church arrangements with spring flowers. They can remain in the arrangement for several weeks with changes of flowers and water. The buds will gradually begin to show signs of life and eventually develop into leaves or flowers.

LIMITED RESOURCES
An economical arrangement of branches with unfurling buds, daffodils and mahonia foliage. Extra branches would make a larger arrangement. Arranger and photographer Ken Loveday.

At different times, depending on the part of the country, the weather, the garden and the variety, the following can be forced into earlier life: magnolia, forsythia, lilac, broom, horse-chestnut, hazel, flowering currant, peach, apple, cherry, pear, willow.

Wild plant material

AVERAGE RESOURCES
Garden, wild and florists' plant material combined − tulips, daffodils, hellebores (in the fruit stage) and pussy willow. Arranger Marjory Ruse. Photographer D. Rendell.

Pussy willow (Goat or Great Willow, Salix caprea) is still in good condition in many parts of the country and wild, garden and florists' plant material can be combined successfully in one arrangement.

Kingcups or Marsh-marigolds are found in ditches and wet green meadows and these are bright and cheerful for small arrangements. They need deep water. Blackthorn with white flowers picked in bud will last for a short while and is quite dramatic and suitable for a country church. The reddish catkins of the Black Poplar can be found during March and April. In June they can be preserved.

This is the best time of the year to search for driftwood tossed up from the sea and lakes and broken down from trees during winter's storms. Later in the year it has either been hidden by undergrowth, found by someone else or burnt in a general tidy-up for summer.

ALTAR FLOWERS

Wedding flowers of white arums and spray chrysanthemums with pink carnations and bergenia leaves supported on a pinholder. Arranger Jean Taylor. Photographer D. Rendell.

Altar flowers, white arums with garden flowers of early viburnum. Arranger Jean Taylor. Photographer D. Rendell.

A simple altar arrangement of white arum lilies may be extended for a wedding with additional flowers from a florist, since they are now less expensive. Two or three stems of single chrysanthemums and/or a few carnations can make a fuller arrangement. The colour scheme can be white, white and yellow, or white and pink, all of which are fresh and pretty. Usually pale-coloured flowers look better with white because the contrast between white and a darker colour can look too strong. Sometimes bright yellow arums are available, in which case a colour scheme of all yellow or of glowing yellow and orange shows up well. Alternatively, viburnum may be out in some gardens and the sweet-smelling flowers combine well with arums.

CHOOSING THE FLOWERS
Although arums last well it is better to buy young ones. A dark spadix and a crepey spathe indicate old age. The centre spadix should be light in colour and the outside white spathe should look firm. Look at the way the stems curve and choose those that you will be able to arrange easily.

Carnations should be tight in the centre and have firm outside petals. Chrysanthemums should have fresh-looking foliage, some buds and flowers with light centres. Those with long branches are easy to cut down into separate stems.

Leaves are necessary for softening the look of bare stems and for concealing the mechanics. Choose those which will be in scale with the flowers, such as the evergreen leaves of bergenia, honesty, laurel, elaeagnus, spotted laurel. Elaeagnus 'Limelight', with yellow splashed leaves, or the silver backs of Elaeagnus macrophylla can be used as a change from all-green leaves. Greens can be varied also from darker green rhododendron to lighter green skimmia leaves.

MAKING THE ARRANGEMENT
The stem ends of arum lilies can be a nuisance because they split easily, and the softness of the tissue usually makes them unsuitable for pushing into Oasis. Wire netting, a pinholder, or the two combined, are better. When stems are long and a little floppy it is necessary to use wire netting as a second support. Splitting can be avoided if the stem ends are bound with soft yarn. Alternatively the stems can be cut sharply before impaling them; if necessary cut again. Another helpful method is to push a cocktail stick or a thin rod into the stem to act as a splint.

If stems are straight and you wish to have curves, the warmth of the hand pressed gently along the stems can induce them to curve.

Spray chrysanthemums are especially useful flowers when they have

LIMITED RESOURCES

Arums in different stages of growth, an arrangement suitable for a modern church. Arum leaves are used as part of the design. Arranger Edith Brack. Photographer Cyril Lindley. By courtesy of Cheshire Life.

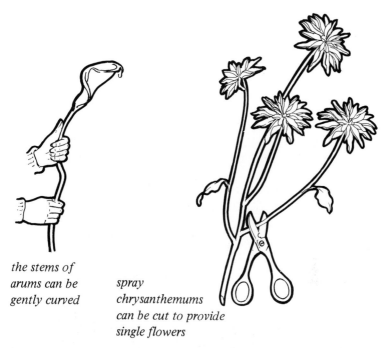

*the stems of
arums can be
gently curved*

*spray
chrysanthemums
can be cut to provide
single flowers*

long branches because these can be cut off and each flower used separately at a different height. This means that fewer stems need be bought. If one flower is left at the top of the main stem it provides height in the arrangement.

Carnations may have slightly floppy stems instead of stiff ones at this time of the year, in which case it is better to use them where they can curve over at the side of the container rather than to try to place them in an upright position.

LIMITED RESOURCES

Country

Daffodils are by now inexpensive to buy and ready to cut in some gardens so they can be used in greater quantities. Forsythia in shades of yellow can be seen growing almost everywhere during this month and long branches can be cut for large arrangements. Some of the stems are stiff and lack grace so, when cutting, search for curved branches because they look more attractive in an arrangement. Cut off some of the side shoots growing at right angles to the main stem because this gives a better line.

Foliage is needed to stretch the flowers and, as a transition between the forsythia and the shorter-stemmed daffodils, evergreens can be used. Variegated leaves give vitality to the arrangement, such as long stems of Euonymus fortunei 'Variegata' with cream and green foliage, variegated ivies, Spotted Laurel or Golden Privet. Plainer, larger leaves, such as rhododendron or laurel, are better for the centre and make a plain background to show up the flowers, as well as providing density.

LIMITED RESOURCES, COUNTRY
White daffodils, yellow forsythia, rhododendron and euonymus foliage in a brass container. Arranger Jean Taylor. Photographer D. Rendell.

Flowers arranged to complement the font in the Baptistery of Guildford Cathedral, by Jane Lee. Photographer Jeremy Hall

Soft colours arranged by Elsie Lamb near the altar in the Lady Chapel, Guildford Cathedral. Photographer Jeremy Hall

The colour scheme of yellow, white and green can be seen easily from a distance.

Mechanics
The stems of all these types of plant material can be impaled easily on a pinholder and a brass container is a colour-link with the yellow flowers. If Oasis is used in the container soft-stemmed daffodils may require the support of a cocktail stick or a woody stem (such as a short length of forsythia) pushed into the stem end. Extra support for the long forsythia stems can be provided by using a cap of wire netting over the top of the pinholder of Oasis.

wire netting provides a second stem support

City
Foliage in March can continue to be a problem for city dwellers but a few spring flowers can be combined with dried and/or preserved plant material and/or a few leaves from a houseplant. As houseplants resume growth from late March onwards two or three leaves should normally be replaced on the plant quite quickly.

Large leaves with a good shape are the most suitable, such as those of long-lasting Monstera deliciosa (Swiss Cheese Plant), Fatsia japonica (Japanese Aralia), Ficus elastica robusta (Rubber Plant) and Aspidistra lurida (Cast Iron Plant).

Fatsia japonica is an excellent shrub for a city garden if it is in a position sheltered from the wind. It tolerates sun or shade and is at its best against a south or west-facing wall. If a local supply is not available for church use it is well worth planting this shrub for its evergreen, large leaves which can be cut all the year round.

LIMITED RESOURCES, CITY

A brown stoneware container lifts the arrangement of everlasting coconut palm spathes, curved inwards to draw attention to the arums and light green leaves of Fatsia japonica on a pinholder. Arranger Nora Willis. Photographer Scott Lauder. By courtesy of The Flower Arranger.

It can also be grown in a pot in the house, but choose a light cool position and avoid a warm room. If the leaves turn yellow and drop off it means that the temperature is too high. Aucuba japonica (Spotted Laurel), which is normally an outdoor plant, can also be grown in the house to provide useful leaves all year. A cool position is again necessary.

IDEA OF THE MONTH

During March the florists' shops are full of pots of small spring flowers and in many warmer parts of the country they begin to appear in gardens, especially towards the end of the month. These gay little flowers are delightful after the long winter months and groupings of many colours combined together look most attractive. Flowers include crocuses, chionodoxas, miniature narcissi, short-stemmed tulips, hyacinths, irises, leucojums, scillas, primulas (including primroses and polyanthuses), muscaris and violets.

These flowers do not last well when cut, but if the root or bulb is retained their life is much longer. Flowers growing in pots can be assembled together in a large container and the gaps filled in with peat. Alternatively the plants can be eased gently from their pots and planted in John Innes No. 2, which should be firmed down around the roots and bulbs. This type of miniature spring garden can be planted in a trough or low bowl containing gravel for drainage. Small-leafed green plants such as ivies and a few plants or bulbs dug from the garden (if they can be spared) can be added to fill in gaps and soften the edge of the container. Make sure the container is deep enough for the bulbs and roots and that there is space to water the plants.

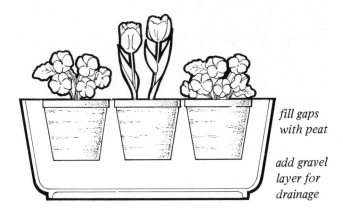

fill gaps with peat

add gravel layer for drainage

You may also want to add cut flowers, such as daffodils, to give height to an otherwise low grouping. Push a small container, painted with dark matt paint, into the compost to hold the mechanics for cut flowers and water in the same way as in a pot-et-fleur (see page 43). When a plant's flowers fade another plant can easily be substituted or cut flowers added to fill the gap.

IDEA OF THE MONTH
Hyacinth bulbs, small ivy plants, rooted primroses and polyanthus with cut daffodils for height in a simulated stone trough. Arranger Jean Taylor. Photographer D. Rendell.

SPECIAL OCCASION FLOWERS

Large arrangements which can be seen by the whole congregation are often needed for special occasions. This is not difficult in April and May when branches of blossom can be cut. And in summer there are many long-stemmed flowers such as delphiniums, peonies, lilies, poppies and angelica. In the autumn there are dahlias and chrysanthemums, large flowers with naturally long stems, and in the winter there is dried and preserved plant material such as Pampas grass and Bells-of-Ireland, and evergreens with long branches to give height.

But in early spring when flowers are short stemmed and small in size tall arrangements can be a problem, especially because people are anxious to see fresh flowers after the sparseness of winter. The solution is to lengthen the stems by artificial means such as by using a tube or cone on a stick (see page 45) or by putting the whole arrangement on a tall pedestal or a built-in shelf or alcove on the church wall. In some churches there is a shelf behind the screen and flowers can be arranged to flow down gracefully from this, using ivies for trails. Brackets attached to the walls are also useful because the flowers can be hung from these and are then seen above the heads of the congregation.

When there are no built-in shelves or brackets, and a change from the familiar pedestal is wanted, then clusters of cones are a good idea. These can be mounted separately on sticks and concealed with evergreens, but too many of them upset the stability of the arrangement. This problem is easily solved by having a foundation constructed to which the cones can be attached firmly. It need not be expensive because little material or work is involved. This foundation, or preferably two of them, can be used over and over again for years to come as a 'column tree'. It makes a tall, slim decoration ideal for flowers with short stems.

Column tree

Method of construction

Buy a wooden stake 2 inches (5 cms) square and of any required length. This needs a firm base on which to stand, but it can be held in position by brackets or angle irons screwed to a 12 inch (30 cms), or larger, square of wood. Alternatively the end of the stake can be supported in a plastic plant pot or bucket, or in an empty paint can, using plaster of Paris for support (see page 123).

Strap several clusters of three or four cones to the stake. If the decoration is to be placed against a wall three cones are sufficient in each

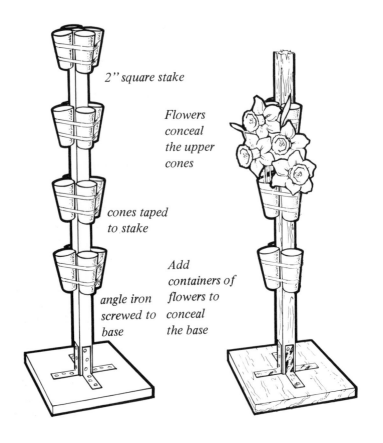

2" square stake

Flowers
conceal
the upper
cones

cones taped
to stake

Add
containers of
angle iron   flowers to
screwed to   conceal
base   the base

cluster, but if the arrangement is to be seen all round then four cones, one on each side of the wooden stake, are advisable. It needs two people to strap on the cones, one to hold them and the other to wind on Sellotape, insulating tape or Oasis tape. This must be done in two places to hold the cones firmly.

The length of the space between each cluster depends on the anticipated length of the flower stems. The shorter the stems the closer should be the clusters of cones. The plant material in one cluster must conceal the cones in the cluster above. If long branches of evergreens are used then the space between the cones can be longer than when spring flowers are predominant. A space as short as 4 inches (10 cms) to 6 inches (15 cms) may be necessary between the top of one group and the bottom of the one above.

When all the cones are firmly strapped on to the stake, spray the construction with matt paint, or brush on a dark-coloured emulsion paint.

If the stake is supported with plaster of Paris in a utilitarian plant pot or bucket this can be placed into an outer, more decorative container. But allow space for mechanics between the plaster and the container's rim, to support plant material to hide the lower part of the stake. If a wooden base is used, one or more containers can be placed on it for flowers. Wire netting or Oasis can be used to support the plant material in the cones. It is important to top them up with water regularly because the small amount they hold is soon taken up by the flowers.

FLOWERS AND FOLIAGE FOR FESTIVALS AND SAINT DAYS

1 March, St David's Day

The day set apart for St David, patron saint of Wales and a symbol of nationhood, was probably chosen because his death may have been on March 1 AD 589. Legend says a host of angels bore his spirit to heaven. David grew up as a Christian and became the Primate of Wales. He founded many churches of which fifty-three bear his name.

Wales has two national emblems, the leek and the daffodil, but in recent years the latter has become more important. This is just as well for church flower arrangers, who might have trouble making an attractive arrangement of leeks.

2 March, John Wesley

John and Charles Wesley are commemorated on this day by the Anglican Church of Canada. During fifty years of evangelism John travelled 250,000 miles on horseback and preached 40,000 sermons. A simple arrangement of wild plant material could symbolize his many travels through country lanes to preach.

17 March, St Patrick's Day

The patron saint of Ireland lived in the fourth century and there are many legends about him. He was the earliest of British saints and the only one whose writings have survived. He travelled throughout Ireland as a Christian missionary founding churches and forming communities. The shamrock is associated with him because, to illustrate his teaching of the Unity of God in the three persons of Father, Son and Holy Ghost, he showed his congregations a shamrock leaf in which three separate parts all belong to one leaf.

Shamrock may be found on sale in some florists' shops around 17 March. But its small size makes it unsuitable for any but a tiny arrangement at the church entrance. An arrangement of fresh evergreens would be suitable to represent Ireland, the Emerald Isle, where beautiful foliage grows in profusion.

Days dependent on the timing of Easter

These days vary with each year and include the three pre-Lenten Sundays, Shrovetide, Lent, Mothering Sunday, Palm Sunday, Easter, Whitsuntide.

SEPTUAGESIMA

Shrovetide is preceded by three Sundays named Septuagesima, Sexagesima and Quinquagesima, which is fifty days before Easter. Blue, significant of heavenly love and unveiling of truth in the English Scheme of Liturgical Colours, is used on these pre-Lenten Sundays in some churches. If blue flowers are desired there are hyacinths, irises and pots of blue cinerarias and hydrangeas at this time.

Lent

Shrovetide ends with Ash Wednesday when the season of Lent begins, ending with Easter. The penitential and solemn season of Lent lasts forty days, not counting Sundays. It is significant of the forty days of fasting and prayer by Jesus in the wilderness, in preparation for His ministry. In some churches flowers are not used during Lent but in others the significance of flowers is maintained as an outward reminder of the wonder of the natural world created by God.

The church emphasizes the need for reflection, meditation, renewal of faith and self-examination at this time. Violet has always been considered a colour significant of these and also of passion and suffering. It is often therefore the chosen colour for Lent.

It is a receding colour in flowers and normally unsuitable for arrangements to be seen from a distance. There are few violet flowers at this time, although it is possible to find mauve tulips, gladioli, freesias, violets and hydrangeas and cinerarias in pots. It is advisable to order these in advance if they are required for a special date.

Where the significant colour is not used, daffodils may be appropriate because another name for them is Lent-lilies from the Old English 'lencten', the spring.

Mothering Sunday

In its early years the Church had a special ordinance requiring priests and people to visit the Mother Church of the district on a specified day. This eventually became associated with family gatherings and reunions, especially of children with their mothers. The name Mothering Sunday was gradually adopted. It is a time when church life focuses on the Mother Church and on family relationships. Mother's Day, which started in America, coincides with Mothering Sunday and it is a time when a family honours the mother, whether churchgoers or not.

Gifts of flowers, often in the form of simple posies, are traditional. Florists now make up posies for sale, but it is also a suitable time to teach children how to make their own from garden flowers, and it could be a good activity for a Sunday School class.

A group from Hale Junior Flower Club making posies for Mothering Sunday. Photographer D. Rendell.

Making a posy

A posy is the modern version of the traditional tussie-mussie carried by both men and women in Tudor times. It was thought that many plants had the power to ward off evil and disease and they were carried when walking in refuse-ridden streets and among sick and dirty people. A tussie-mussie was a simple bunch of flowers preferably sweet-smelling. Early Victorian ladies also carried posies, but these were neat and regular, often of circles of flowers surrounded by a frill of leaves or lace and held in a holder made for the stems. The holders were often very beautiful and made of precious metal. A long pin was attached for holding the stems firmly and a chain and ring for placing on a lady's belt so that she could drop the posy when her hands were needed for other things.

A modern version of garden flowers for children to make can start with a large central flower with other flowers added around it in circles of one variety, binding the stems together gradually with yarn, Sellotape or thin wire. Make a hole in the centre of a paper doily and slip the stems through it, binding them with ribbon or floral tape. Make sure the flowers are well conditioned before they are made into a posy because they will be without water for some time.

Small dried flowers in a Victorian posy holder. Arranger Ilona Barney. Photographer Dennis Barnard. By courtesy of The Flower Arranger.

74

19 March, St Joseph; 23 March, St Benedict

These are two saints that could have interpretative flower arrangements made for them. St Joseph, the carpenter of Nazareth, is the patron saint of those who work with their hands. An arrangement of flowers with beautiful craftwork would be appropriate.

Poverty, chastity and stability were the early vows taken by monks led by Benedict and an interpretative arrangement could be made which would be significant, using simple and sparse plant material.

FORWARD PLANNING

Perennials to plant

Hardy perennials to produce flowers and leaves for cutting later in the year should be planted by the end of the month, whenever the weather is suitable and the ground soft enough. In colder parts of the country April is better for some plants. There are many hardy perennials to choose from but the following short and reliable selection is useful and a basis from which to extend a collection for church arrangements. The botanical names are shown for safety in ordering plants. Ferns and grasses are also included.

Round and daisy-type flowers

Peonies	Paeonia lactiflora hybrids, double-flowered varieties 'Sarah Bernhardt' bright pink, 'Bower of Roses' rose-crimson, 'Solange' cream-buff, 'La Cygne' white. Single flowers – 'Dresden' blush-white, 'Globe of Light' pale pink, May-June.
Poppies	Papaver orientale 'Mrs Perry' pink, 'Perry's White', 'Marcus Perry' orange-scarlet, May-June.
Scabious	Scabiosa caucasica 'Clive Greaves' mauve, 'Miss Willmott' white, 'Moonstone' light blue, June-September.
Yarrow	Achillea filipendulina 'Gold Plate' is a good colour and dries well for winter with flat dense heads, July-September. Cut for drying when mature.
Agapanthus	Headbourne Hybrids are generally hardy with deep violet-blue to pale blue spherical umbels, July-August.
Globe artichokes	Cynara scolymus and cardoons, C. cardunculus, big globe heads with thistle-like flowers August-

75

	September; dry for winter use.
Shasta daises	Chrysanthemum maximum 'Esther Read' or 'Wirral Supreme' double white and singles 'Everest' and 'H.Siebert', June-August.
Cone-flowers	Rudbeckia fulgida 'Deamii' or 'Goldsturm' yellows with dark eyes, July-September.
Leopard's Bane	Doronicum cordatum 'Harpur Crewe' or 'Spring Beauty' yellow, April-May.
Heleniums	Helenium autumnale 'Mahogany' gold and brown-red, 'Latest Red' bronze-red, 'Golden Youth' yellow, August-October.
Gaillardias	'Croftway Yellow', 'Wirral Flame', June-July.
Pyrethrums	'E.M. Robinson' pink, 'Marjorie Robinson' deep pink, 'Brenda' cerise, 'Evenglow' salmon, June–July.
Japanese anemones	Anemone japonica 'September Charm' single pink, 'Queen Charlotte' semi-double pink, 'White Queen'.

Flowers for height

Acanthus	Acanthus mollis latifolius or A. spinosus, purple and white flowers, dries for winter use. July-August.
Monkshood	Aconitum arendsii blue, A. lycoctonum yellow-green, August.
Bellflowers	Campanula lactiflora 'Loddon Anna' pink, 'Prichard's Variety' violet-blue, 'Alba' white, June-July.
Euphorbia	Euphorbia characias and E. wulfenii for a yellow-green bushy stem, May-July.
Bugbane	Cimicifuga racemosa, white, August.
Red-hot Poker	Kniphofia. there are many, to provide flowers from June to October: 'Shining Sceptre' clear yellow, 'Maid of Orleans' ivory-cream, 'Brimstone' late, deep yellow, 'Samuel's Sensation' scarlet, 'Earliest of All' an early flame, 'Bee's Sunset' orange.
Plume Poppy	Macleaya cordata 'Coral Plume' small flowers, long stems, June–August.

Mullein	Verbascum hybridum 'Golden Bush' bright yellow, 'C.L. Adams' deep yellow, 'Gainsborough' pale yellow.
Crambe	Crambe cordifolia, very tall stems of small white flowers, June-July.
Astilbes	Astilbe x arendsii 'Bressingham Beauty' pink, 'Cologne' deeper pink, 'Deutschland' white, June-August.
Michaelmas daisies	Aster novi-belgii in pinks, reds, mauves and white, September-October.
Bearded irises	with a huge colour range in May-June.
Lupins	Russell hybrids in many colours, May-July.
Globe artichokes and cardoons	previously described.
Delphiniums	in blues, pinks, white; Belladonna varieties are easier to arrange because they are shorter in stem, but the taller Pacific hybrids are magnificent for big arrangements. Blue Fountain, a new strain, is compact and only 2½-3 feet tall, June-July.

Plants for foliage

The hostas have especially valuable leaves for flower arrangers. There are many varieties and all are useful, In particular H. sieboldiana 'Elegans' blue-green large leaves, H. fortunei 'Albopicta' lime-green with yellow edge turning plain green later, H. fortunei 'Aureomarginata' yellow edged, H. crispula, dark green with white margins, H. x 'Thomas Hogg' cream edged, H. ventricosa and H.v. 'Variegata'. The leaves can be used from late May (early May in some places) to late summer.

Bergenias are just as useful as hostas and are evergreen. In winter they are often shot with red and yellow, but they are available all year and provide an excellent plain background for flowers. B. crassifolia has spoon-shaped leaves, B. cordifolia leaves are heart-shaped, B. purpurascens, syn B. delavayi, turns a good colour, the hybrid 'Ballawley' has very large leaves. Plain green leaves will turn reddish if the stem is cut half through and left for a week or so. Leaves of varying size can be found on all plants.

New Zealand Flax, Phormium tenax, has strap-shaped leaves up to 10 feet. The plain form rather than P.t. 'Purpureum' or P.t. 'Variegatum' should be planted in colder places, evergreen.

Solomon's Seal, Polygonatum x hybridum, arching stems, May to late summer.

Euphorbia robbiae for rosettes of leaves almost all the year round.

Tellima grandiflora, evergreen, but the thin, small leaves turn bronze in winter.

Globe artichokes and cardoons, previously described, for dramatic arched foliage in summer.

Leaves of flag irises are useful for a long period. Iris pseudacorus 'Variegata' is a water iris which grows 3-4 feet in a pool but only to 2 feet in a border, but the lime-green and yellow striped leaves are distinctive when new; later they turn plain green. Iris pallida has tall green leaves and 'Variegata' is marked with primrose.

Crocosmia masonorum with sword-like leaves in summer, often included under Antholyza and sometimes under Montbretia.

Helleborus corsicus with useful green leaves, especially in winter.

Pachysandra terminalis, a hardy evergreen ground cover, long-lasting in water, slow to start.

Periwinkle, Vinca major 'Variegata' with trails to use all year.

Osumda regalis, 'The Royal Fern', a hardy fern to cut when mature, good for pressing.

Polystichum setiferum 'Divisilobum' a beautiful hardy fern.

Pampas grass, Cortaderia selloana 'Pumila' is more compact form for a smaller garden.

Miscanthus sinensis 'Variegatus' a tall striped grass, April-November.

Extras for filling in

Globe thistle, Echnicops ritro, spherical blue heads, dry easily.

Sea hollies, especially Eryngium alpinum with fluffy heads that glycerine well, E. giganteum, a tall variety which dies after flowering but the stems preserve with glycerine.

Chinese Lantern, Physalis franchettii with orange seedpods in autumn.

Alstroemeria 'Ligtu Hybrids', orange colours in June.

Burning Bush, Dictamnus albus, white flower spikes in June-July.

Euphorbia polychroma, small but brilliant yellow flowers in early spring.

Phlox, many varieties and colours but white is especially useful for church arrangements in July-August. 'White Admiral', 'Mother of Pearl' soft pink, 'Vintage Wine' purple-red, 'Sandringham' cyclamen-pink with darker centre, 'Prince of Orange' orange-salmon.

Phytolacca americana, green berries turning to dark purple after white flowers, June-September.

Golden Rod, Solidago 'Golden Shower', or 'Golden Gates', July–August.

Globe Flowers, Trollius 'Goldquelle' or 'Canary Bird' yellow, June.

Sedum spectabile 'Autumn Joy' and S. maximum 'Atropurpureum'. The former can be used when the heads are green in August, shading red gradually until October when they are dark red. The latter grows taller than most sedums. One of the most useful plants for flower arrangers because of the rough-textured heads and equally valuable foliage, both long-lasting.

Thalictrum speciosissimum, tall with fluffy yellow flowers. T. dipterocarpum 'Album', tall fluffy white flowers, June-August.

Lady's Mantle, Alchemilla mollis, small lime-green flowers, small round green leaves, June-August.

Bleeding Heart, Dicentra spectabilis, short arching sprays of small flowers, May-June.

Bell Flower, Campanula persicifolia 'Telham Beauty', blue cups. C. latifolia 'Gloaming' pale blue, June-July.

Lilies
Lilies are especially suitable for church arrangements. They have large, long-lasting flowers in beautiful colours and excellent form which shows up well from a distance. Lilium candidum is the Madonna Lily seen in so many Renaissance paintings and a symbol of the Madonna. It is also called the Cottage Garden Lily. Outdoor lilies should be planted between October and March, setting each bulb two and a half times deeper than its height, except shallow-planted L. candidum, in beds containing plenty of well-rotted compost. Garden centres carry many varieties, so watch for their arrival, and flowering is generally between July and September. L. regale is a very hardy white with wine-coloured reverse; the American Mid-Century Hybrids are reliable. 'Enchantment' orange, 'Destiny' yellow with brown spots, 'Cinnabar' maroon red and the Aurelian Hybrids 'Pink Perfection' and 'Green Magic'.

Gladioli
Another invaluable flower for the church arrangements in many

colours. The corms should be planted from mid-March to late April, depending on the weather, at fortnightly intervals for a succession of bloom. Plant 4–6 inches deep (10–15 cms) 6–9 inches (15–22.5 cms) apart, with a cane for support inserted at the same time. Sharp sand beneath the corm improves drainage and prevents rotting. Water well once a week. The large-flowered gladioli are invaluable for a church, but Butterfly and Primulinus varieties are useful for smaller arrangements.

Details of cultivation and illustrations can be found in books such as the *Readers' Digest Encyclopaedia of Garden Plants and Flowers, Flower Arranging in House and Garden* by George Smith published by Pelham Books, *Flower Arranging from your Garden* by Sheila Macqueen, published by Ward Lock, *The Bulb Book* by Frederic Doerflinger, published by David & Charles, *Pictorial Gardening* published by Collingridge, *Perennials for your Garden* by Alan Bloom, published by Floraprint Ltd., *Readers' Digest Gardening Year.*

APRIL

This can be a busy time for the church flower arranger if Easter falls in April, but to make life easier the occasional warm sunshine, in an otherwise moist and cloudy month, hurries on the garden flowers and blossom.

Spring is spreading rapidly across the country and while some people consider February, March and April to be the spring months, others regard them as March, April and May. Either way April is spring for everyone, although there is still a considerable difference between the weather conditions in the north and south of the country and from day to day. Frost and snow are possible in some areas but periods of southerly winds and warmer rains from the west hasten the growth in the garden. Many people feel a sense of joy because life is awakening in growing trees and plants and the spring flowers are much enjoyed.

PLANT MATERIAL

Florists' Flowers

Spring daffodils, tulips, freesias, lilacs, arums and clivias intermingle with flowers more often associated with summer such as stocks, gladioli, sweet peas, lilies, gerberas, alstroemerias, antirrhinums and blue agapanthuses. It is one of the best months in the year for choice in the shops and there are many good buys.

Pots of flowering hydrangeas, cinerarias, cyclamens and azaleas are still available and the foliage of box, cupressus, rhododendron, laurel, pittosporum, pine, grevillea and eucalyptus are often in stock.

It is not necessary to take a lot of trouble over the conditioning of shop flowers. They will have been prepared and placed in water after their travels by the florist. Cut flowers sold by the trade are chosen for their long-lasting quality and are unlikely to wilt. However, on arrival home it is always better to remove the wrappings and loosen the ties at once. Then snip off the ends of the stems and place them in a bucket of tepid water until you are ready to take the flowers to arrange in the church. This is much better for the flowers than leaving them to lie about in their wrappings without water.

Garden Plant Material

Foliage

Leaves, which are invaluable for stretching a few flowers into a big arrangement, are still limited to evergreens. Young foliage may be appearing in the gardens but wilts quickly when cut and it is inadvisable to use it for a church arrangement at this time. It is usually not sufficiently mature to take up water and remain firm until mid or late May at the earliest. As an alternative to evergreens, glycerined foliage in shades of brown can be used, such as preserved beech that has been lightened to a soft tan colour by standing it in the sun. It looks daintier than evergreens and is attractive with the paler coloured spring flowers. Long branches of glycerined beech can be used to make a large arrangement, with a few fresh flowers in the centre.

Branches

The great joy of the garden in April is the unfolding of leaf and flower buds on the trees. Long branches can be cut for huge arrangements. These should be picked when in bud or slightly showing colour because then they will open rapidly in a warm room. Open flowers soon shed their petals, making the church look untidy. All woody stems last longer if about 3 inches (7.5 cms) of outer bark is scraped off, using a small knife. Then split the stem ends for about 2 inches (5 cms), using flower scissors or secateurs, before placing them in deep tepid water. A large polythene bag can be placed over the top of the branches to conserve moisture if they are not to be used at once, but take care to avoid knocking off any buds. If the buds are tightly closed leave the bucket in a warm room, but if not, put it in a cool outhouse.

Trimming is usually necessary to provide a pleasing line without strong side shoots to divert the main movement of the branch. Some flowering branches are sufficiently laden with flowers to make an

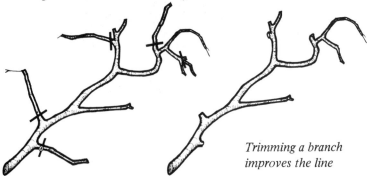

Trimming a branch improves the line

AVERAGE RESOURCES *Five tulips, one particularly opened, fourteen narcissi with bulrushes for height, pale glycerined beech and evergreen elaeagnus and yew with pine cones for a contrast of texture. The arrangement could also be made in a low bowl. Arranger Renee Mottershead. By courtesy of Lancashire Life.*

LIMITED RESOURCES *Magnolia flowers with leaves of Arum italicum to soften the bare branch and hide the mechanics makes a simple arrangement for a modern or country church. Arranger Sybil Goer. Photography M.R. Hulme.*

arrangement on their own without other plant material. Barer branches may need softening at the point where they enter the container and a few evergreen leaves or those of arums or bergenias can be used. Short-stemmed cut flowers together with long branches for height can make a lovely spring arrangement.

Flowering branches that can be used in April and May include those of Prunus, a genus containing many of the most popular spring-flowering ornamentals — almonds, plums, cherries and crab apples. There are also the flowering branches of pears and plums, if one can forgo the fruit.

Magnolia, with its magnificent pink-tinted ivory flowers opening before the leaves, is lovely to use in church providing a long-lasting flower arrangement is not necessary, but if someone during the week can cut away the faded flowers the buds will continue to open.

The early rhododendrons should be picked in tight bud, just showing colour, because the flowers open quickly. Forsythias and viburnums are still available in colder parts of the country.

Foliage branches include the lovely amber-pink Acer pseudoplatanus 'Brilliantissimum' which turns green later. It is one of the few acers with leaves that do not wilt when cut and it looks beautiful with pink, orange or white tulips against stone walls. It is a slow-growing tree but well worth planting because a mature tree provides branches of great beauty. Whitebeam (Sorbus aria) has leaves of white-green in spring. They look clean and fresh and combine well with pastel spring flowers. Later the leaves become a darker green. It is a tree which grows to 15-20 feet (5-6 metres). The leaves preserve well with glycerine, becoming dark brown with a grey underside.

Perennials
The first of the useful perennial and sub-shrubby flowers begin to appear. These include Euphorbia polychroma with bright yellow-green heads of bracts which are excellent for filling in and a good colour for a church arrangement.

The yellow daisy-type flowers of doronicums last well in water while the flowers of bergenias in pink and white provide a strong stem of medium height. They can be combined with pink carnations for a change from the usual yellows of spring. Dicentra spectabilis with small pink flowers and graceful arching stems is also available at this time of the year. Cytisus praecox, an early bloom with cream flowers, is useful for curves.

Bulb flowers

Narcissi and hyacinths are still available in many gardens but this is tulip time, with flowers of many colours. The stems can be awkward, changing position overnight, and are better arranged in informal designs or with short stems. Open tulips with dramatic centres make excellent emphasis flowers. They can be opened with your hand if they are sufficiently mature. Using your thumb, gently stroke the petals back, one-by-one, on to your first finger. If they do not turn back easily the flowers are too young and are better left closed. Two or three open flowers can make an effective centre in an arrangement of spring branches and leaves.

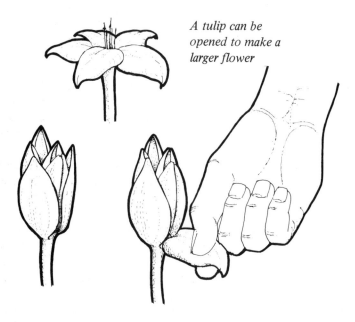

A tulip can be opened to make a larger flower

There are many colours in tulips from which to choose, but the brighter colours show up better in the dimmer lighting of a church. Yellows or white combine well with yellow or white blossom; white or pink with white or pink blossom; any colour, but especially red, looks attractive with unfurling green leaves. Orange tulips look unusual with pink blossom and harmonize easily with yellow or white blossom.

The Crown Imperial (Fritillaria imperialis) in yellow or amber is a distinctive bulb flower often seen in the early Flemish and Dutch flower paintings and elegant for present-day arrangements, especially of mixed spring flowers.

Orchids

Amateur growers may have sprays of greenhouse orchids to spare for the church in April and onwards. They are regarded as an exotic flower in this country, but in addition to their distinctive beauty they are extremely long-lasting as a cut flower and so well worth using in an arrangement. They tend to look better used in sprays combined with glycerined foliage, driftwood or branches at this time of year. They do not mix well with other flowers.

Wild Plant Material

One of the loveliest flowering branches for use in church at this time is Acer platanoides (Norway Maple). From a distance the brilliant lime-green flowers can be mistaken for leaves, but the massed bunches of tiny flowers appear two to three weeks before the leaves. The tall-growing vigorous trees grow in some gardens and can often be found on a roadside.

Horsechestnut buds (sticky buds) are found in many places and, although the stems are stiff, it is fascinating to watch the leaves gradually unfurl in an arrangement. They can be combined with spring flowers and some evergreen leaves to conceal the mechanics.

Wild daffodils, primroses, cowslips, fritillaries and white dead-nettle (Adam and Eve in the Bower) are abundant in some areas but are only suitable for small arrangements. In places they are rare and should not be picked.

Leaves of the wild arum (Lords and Ladies) grow near ditches and the Pasque Flower can be found in chalk and limestone areas. Pasque means Easter and the flower's purple-red petals were thought to grow from human blood. However, the flower is unusually scarce and should not be picked nowadays.

Branches of wild cherry can be found but should be picked in tight bud because the flowers open quickly. In late March and early April there are white flowers on the blackthorn, but they do not last well and are prickly to cut. The alders bear reddish catkins but they are not spectacular for an arrangement when viewed from a distance in a church.

The young sycamore leaf is most useful. It is bronze and makes a beautiful background for pink, cream, orange or flame-coloured tulips. The leaves keep well when cut if they are placed immediately in a bucket of water and not removed from water for more than a minute or two at any time. They grow in many places and there is no need to conserve them because cutting encourages more growth.

ALTAR FLOWERS

A pair of arrangements is often used on an altar or communion table. However, it is important that because of their size or height they do not dominate the cross, or take up too much of the available space. Simplicity, elegance and smaller-scaled arrangements are often required.

Attention can be directed towards the cross by the use of a curving design such as a crescent or a Hogarth curve. If a pair of arrangements face in opposite ways the cross becomes the focal point of the altar.

Before you begin to make a pair of arrangements, divide the plant material into two separate bunches with similar flowers and foliage in each, so that you do not run short of material for the second arrangement.

There are many branches with flowers or fresh new leaves to provide height and elegant curves in April. It is not possible to make attractive curved designs with straight stemmed material. When cutting branches look for those with pleasing curves, and remember that opposite but similar curves are needed for a pair of arrangements.

Mechanics

Oasis standing an inch or two above the top of the container provides an easy method of obtaining a downward flowing curve. This is not possible in a tall vase with a pinholder, but it can be managed with wire netting if naturally strongly curved plant material is used so that the stem end will be in water. Often careful trimming can produce a sharply curved branch for this purpose.

Flat leaves such as those of Spotted Laurel, honesty, Arum italicum and the bergenias, or the clustered foliage of Choisya ternata or Euphorbia robbiae can be used to conceal the mechanics. A few spring flowers can be used for emphasis in the centre of the arrangement.

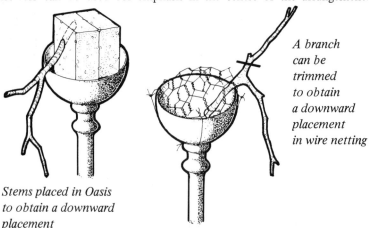

A branch can be trimmed to obtain a downward placement in wire netting

Stems placed in Oasis to obtain a downward placement

ALTAR FLOWERS *Whitebeam provides a gentle crescent shape for one of a pair of arrangements. Small bergenia leaves conceal the foam standing above the container's rim. Three stems of single chrysanthemums cut down provide emphasis. Arranger Jean Taylor. Photographer D. Rendell.*

LIMITED RESOURCES

Country

A large arrangement can be made with little or no cost at this time of the year using garden and wild plant material, such as flowering and leafy branches and spring bulb flowers.

A spring pedestal arrangement

Spring flowers are smaller than those of summer and autumn when peonies, roses, dahlias and chrysanthemums can be cut, so more plant material is needed.

Mechanics

Oasis is ideal for making a pedestal arrangement because the stems can be angled easily. But, because of their softness, daffodil stems may not be suitable for Oasis, and wire netting combined with a pinholder may be necessary.

(a) *Oasis*

Stand one whole soaked block of Oasis upright in the container with a half block in front of it. The container can be a cake-baking tin painted with dark matt paint, or any other receptacle that holds plenty of water. Remember that the many flowers and leaves used in a pedestal arrangement take up the available water quickly. The half block of Oasis should stand above the rim of the container for about 3-4 inches (7.5-8 cms) so that stems can be inserted to flow downwards. If the container is too deep to allow this then the level of the Oasis can be raised with an upturned flower saucer, old Oasis blocks or gravel.

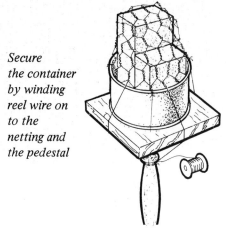

*Secure
the container
by winding
reel wire on
to the
netting and
the pedestal*

LIMITED RESOURCES, COUNTRY *Lime-green Norway maple flowers with ivy trails provide the outline for a background of daffodils and Spotted Laurel to hide the wire netting. Arranger Jean Taylor. Photographer D. Rendell.*

To secure the Oasis place a cap of 1 inch (2.5 cms) wire netting over the top and down the sides. Fasten this in place by winding a length of reel wire or string to one side of the netting, twist it around the pedestal and tie it on the other side of the netting. Do this again from the centre front to the centre back. Make sure that the Oasis is held firmly but that the netting does not cut deeply into it. If necessary add one or more lengths of reel wire for extra security. The pedestal, container and mechanics should then be firm and the container cannot be pushed off the pedestal's shelf.

When a pedestal arrangement is used near an aisle or where people will brush past it, it may be necessary for stability to wire the stem of the pedestal to a pew end or other permanent furnishing.

(b)   *Wire netting*

When wire netting is used instead of Oasis, a heavy pinholder is needed in the bottom of the container. The tallest central stems can be impaled on this to position them and also to hold the netting in place. A slightly shallower container, than the deep type used for Oasis is advisable; about 4 inches (10 cms) is tall enough. Otherwise it is difficult to allow plant material to flow downwards over the rim.

Make a large mound of crumpled 2 inch (5 cms) wire netting so that about 6 inches (15 cms) of it appears above the rim of the container. Wire the netting to the pedestal as described for Oasis.

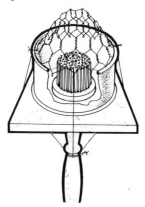

Making the arrangement

Flower arrangers can make a pedestal in a number of ways and it makes little difference to the end result. If you are a beginner you will probably find it easier to establish first the height and width of the design by placing branches in the centre and at the lower sides. Then conceal the mechanics and the container with short-stemmed flat leaves. Add emphasis flowers and additional branches and foliage as necessary to complete the arrangement.

The design often looks more unified when some of the branches are carried through the centre of the arrangement. When the front of the design is to your liking take a look at the back and the sides to see if any more filling in is necessary.

When the arrangement is complete walk to the back of the church to see the effect, but make as few changes as possible because one change often leads to another.

The stems of spring flowers are short and it may be necessary, for transitional height between the flowers and the branches, to use taller stemmed gladioli or lilies, or to place short-stemmed flowers into tubes bound to sticks (see page 45).

City

The simplicity of a few spring flowers can be quite beautiful in a small city church. Weathered wood or budding branches can be used to frame and emphasize the flowers and this enlarges the arrangement.

A pinholder is normally the easiest type of mechanic to use but it can be difficult when placed at the bottom of a tall vase. It can be lifted nearer to the rim by filling the vase to within about 3 inches (6.5 cms) of the top with sand, gravel or even newspaper crumpled up tightly and well packed down. Fill the vase with water until this stands above the pinholder.

water level

Sand

Some flowers, such as amaryllis or arums, need evergreen leaves from a florist or town garden to soften the bare appearance of their stems. Flowers such as daffodils, irises and tulips have attached leaves and other foliage may not be necessary.

One large amaryllis or a single stem of lilies can be used in the centre of the design but several stems of smaller spring flowers are usually

LIMITED RESOURCES, CITY *An economical arrangement for a small city church. The driftwood can remain in position with a change of flowers. Arranger Joan Ewing. Photography Peter Harding. By courtesy of* The Flower Arranger.

necessary. Cut the stems to different lengths and place the flowers at different angles so that the shape of each one can be seen clearly. This style of design looks more attractive when the stem ends are placed close together on the pinholder instead of being set apart.

IDEA OF THE MONTH

A daffodil tree

There is often an abundance of daffodils at this time of year and their brilliant yellow colouring is especially striking in a gloomy corner.

A foundation stand can easily be constructed with a length of wood 1½ inches (3.7 cms) square and of any desired length, such as about 6½ feet (2.5 m). Set the end of the wood in an empty paint tin about 7 inches (17.5 cms) in height and diameter, using cement or plaster of Paris. Screw four 3 inch (7.5 cms) right angle irons at intervals down

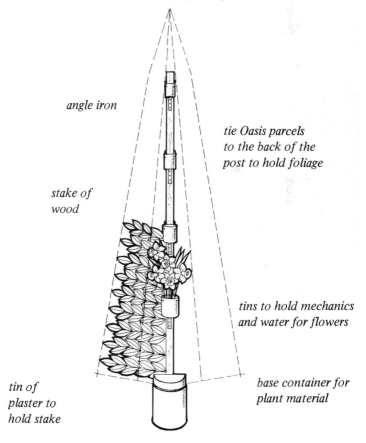

angle iron

tie Oasis parcels
to the back of the
post to hold foliage

stake of
wood

tins to hold mechanics
and water for flowers

tin of
plaster to
hold stake

base container for
plant material

one face of the post and place tins on these to hold crumpled wire netting or Oasis. The tins can be held in position with binding tape, or with wire threaded through two holes (made with a hammer and a nail) placed under the rim of each tin, and wound on to staples on either side of the post. Place a larger tin or a semi-circular plastic container on the base tin. The basic construction should be painted with dark green matt emulsion paint to camouflage it.

Cut large blocks of Oasis in half lengthways, soak and parcel them in thin plastic bags. Secure these with garden string to the back of the post, all the way up. The foundation is then ready for adding plant material. Begin with branches of laurel or other evergreens pushed into the bags to make a triangular background of foliage. To the centre add daffodils and shorter sprays of leaves to hide the tins, forming a second triangle of gold within the outer green one. If the base tin shows, add a container at floor level for laurel leaves. Garden daffodils can be used or about eight bunches of shop flowers. This is an economical decoration but large and dramatic in effect.

SPECIAL OCCASION FLOWERS

On special occasions when the church is full, or when it is especially desirable for the flowers to be seen, it is better to raise them in some way. Many churches have invested in alabaster or stone plinths, or in iron pedestals made by blacksmiths.

When money is available it may be used to buy one or two especially beautiful tall supports to provide height. These can be inspiring to the flower arranger and a change from some of the vases in store, such as the white ceramic, boat-shape which is so difficult to use. Experienced members of the church flower guild can be asked to search local auction sales and antique shops for suitable objects. They should look for attractive columns or stems because it is a simple job to convert the top to hold a container.

Tall candlesticks can be found with bowls at the top to catch dripping wax. These can hold instead a block of Oasis or crumpled wire netting, with or without candles. A standard lamp made of carved wood, brass or iron provides good height and can be converted to a flower stand by removing the electrical fittings and replacing them with a wooden shelf of about 10 inches (25 cms) by 8 inches (20 cms). This can hold a baking tin or bowl for mechanics and plant material.

Sometimes candelabras can be bought in which candlecups can be placed for mechanics and flowers. Each holder may be used for separate arrangements or the flowers can be merged to give the appearance of

Flowers arranged by George Smith flanking the font in the Crypt of York Minster. Photographer Lawrence Hill, Warren Jepson & Co. Ltd., Leeds

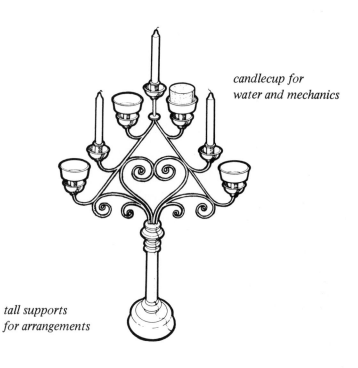

candlecup for
water and mechanics

tall supports
for arrangements

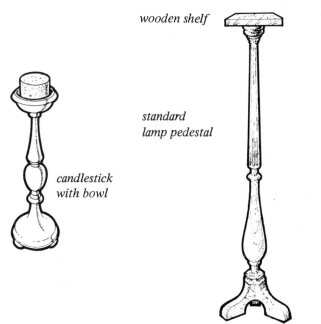

wooden shelf

standard
lamp pedestal

candlestick
with bowl

one arrangement. Candles can be used or not. When these are pushed into Oasis it is better to make a hole first with a small knife and remove a section. This makes the candle secure. It should be put in position before arranging the flowers.

GOOD RESOURCES *An antique stone candlestick with a bowl fixed temporarily to the top for a block of foam and wire netting, well wired together. Garden cherry blossom and hyacinth with florists' lilies, single chrysanthemums and Western hemlock, used on the grey side, arranged by Jean Taylor. Photography D. Rendell.*

Candlecups do not hold sufficient water or Oasis for much plant material and it is better to use a bigger bowl or tin. This can be attached permanently, using a strong adhesive, to the top of the candlestick, or temporarily using Florafix or Oasis fix. In this case it is advisable to use a cap of wire netting over the Oasis and several lengths of reel wire, pulled tightly round the candlestick (see pedestal arrangement page 91) to make sure the container does not slip off.

FLOWERS AND FOLIAGE FOR FESTIVALS AND SAINT DAYS

Palm Sunday, the Sunday before Easter

This day commemorates the entry of Jesus into Jerusalem riding on the back of a donkey. The crowds of people, gathered to celebrate the Jewish Passover, waved olive branches and palm which was carried in ancient times as a symbol of victory or triumph and is still used on festival occasions. These were also strewed in front of Jesus.

The palm of the scriptures is the date palm Phoenix dactylifera with pinnate mid-green leaves up to 6 feet (about 2 m) long. It is not indigenous to this country because it requires a temperature never less than 55°F and therefore substitutes for palm and olive have been used in ceremonies here for centuries. The most common has been willow which is out at this time of the year. It is often called 'palm' because of this symbolic association.

When British life was more rural, country-folk cut long stems of willow and box on Palm Saturday, an activity called 'a-palming'. Houses were decorated with them and processions carried branches into the churches to re-enact the story of Palm Sunday. Flowers and willow were also strewn to make a path for the processions.

There are many plants with the vernacular name of 'palm' but traditionally in this country it is Salix caprea, the goat willow, golden with male catkins or 'goslings'. The female catkins are less spectacular and grow on separate bushes.

With the present-day world-wide exchange of dried plant material date palm fronds may be imported from warmer countries for use at this time. They are beige and not the normal dark green. Cycas leaves, about 2 feet (70 cms) long, are also available. They are not palms although they look like the date palm and are beige when dried, dark brown when glycerined and sometimes dark green from added dye. They can be obtained from florists and flower clubs' sales tables.

Sabal minor, commonly called palmetto, grows wild in warmer countries such as Bermuda and the southern states of America. It has a leaf shaped like a fan and can be trimmed with scissors to a variety of

GOOD RESOURCES *An arrangement suitable for Easter of lilies, dried palmetto and palm spathes with leaves of Fatsia japonica in brown, white and green and called Exultation. Arranger Mrs F. Bickley. Photography D. Rendell. By courtesy of The Flower Arranger.*

shapes. It dries easily and is imported. The leaves are often used by flower arrangers to interpret the sun's rays, triumph, rejoicing, victory or exultation.

Both our native willow and dried cycas, palm or palmetto leaves can be arranged for Palm Sunday with fresh spring flowers but if Easter is late the willow may be past its best. Salix babylonica, Weeping Willow, is beautiful but wilts quickly when cut, making it unsuitable for church arrangements.

Maundy Thursday

This is the traditional name for the Thursday before Easter and is said to be a corruption of 'Mandati', *Dies Mandati* (the Day of the Commandment), referring to the night of Jesus's commandment to his disciples to love one another. In washing their feet Christ performed the most menial task to teach the lesson of humility.

During the Middle Ages bishops, abbots and noblemen washed the feet of the poor on Maundy Thursday in imitation of Christ's act. English sovereigns washed the feet of as many old men as the sovereign's years of age but all that remains of this ceremony, which began in the reign of Edward III, 1327-76, is the bestowing of gifts to the poor. It is often held in Westminster Abbey and special minted silver coins are distributed by the monarch in the nave. All those taking part in the ceremony carry posies of flowers which in earlier days were supposed to be a protection against the plague.

Sometimes Maundy Thursday is called Green Thursday, because of the custom of providing penitents, who had made their confessions on Ash Wednesday, with green branches on this day; this indicated that penance had been completed and they were received back into full church membership.

If any significant decorations are wanted in church on this day, green branches or simple posies of flowers would be appropriate.

Good Friday

This day commemorates the trial and crucifixion of Jesus and most churches are left undecorated. If flowers are wanted, simple white arums or Lilium longiflorum would be suitable.

Easter

The greatest and most joyous festival of the Christian Church commemorates the resurrection of Christ, historically corresponding to the Jewish Passover. The date of Easter changes because it is the first Sunday after the first calendar full moon which happens on, or next after, the spring equinox, 21 March. Therefore it may fall on any date between 21 March and 25 April. Colloquially the term 'Easter' is applied to the week beginning with Easter Sunday.

Easter is the oldest of the Christian festivals and has been observed continuously since Christianity first came to Britain. Bede derives the word 'Easter' from *Eostre* (Eastre), a pagan goddess whose festival was held at the spring equinox. It is said that the Christian Church took this time when 'the old festival was observed with the gladness of a new solemnity'.

Pasche or Pace is the Passover, or Easter, hence the word 'paschal' belonging to this time.

Traditional customs vary from church to church for flower decoration at Easter but arum lilies are used on many altars. Most churches are full of flowers as an expression of joy. Instead of many small arrangements it can be a change to have a few larger ones. The basic constructions described under 'Idea of the month' for March and April are suitable for the shorter stemmed flowers of spring.

Hanging baskets, hung from wall brackets or existing nails, with plenty of trailing ivies, could be a change from the often-seen pedestal arrangements. White and yellow are the traditional colours for Easter flowers and there are florists' lilies, daffodils and narcissi, irises, tulips, lilacs, double freesias, single chrysanthemums, roses, carnations, gladioli, gerbera and from the garden, viburnum, forsythia, broom, hyacinths, tulips, azaleas, irises, camellias, daffodils and narcissi — depending on the date of Easter. All these flowers can be combined with fresh evergreen foliage, dried and glycerined leaves and branches.

A paschal candle is sometimes blessed and placed on the altar or nearby. It has five grains of incense inserted in the form of a cross and remains lit for forty days, until the Ascension. It may be agreed that the paschal candle can be surrounded with flowers (see *Flowers in Church* page 109) which is a charming idea. However the candle is very heavy and needs adequate support. A blacksmith can make a bowl containing a metal tube to hold the candle, on a pedestal. At other times it can be used for flowers alone.

The egg has for centuries been regarded as the symbol of life and the present custom of giving decorated eggs at Easter is an old one. In the Middle Ages the day was sometimes called Egg Sunday and hard-boiled eggs were blessed, given as gifts and called paschal eggs. A basket of eggs would not be inappropriate to use with flowers for an Easter decoration.

Tansy, Tanacetum vulgare, with golden buttons and fern-like leaves could be used in a small flower arrangement. Tansy cakes were made in rural Britain as a remembrance of the bitter herbs eaten by the Jews at the Passover. Thomas Cogan explained in *The Haven of Health,* 1584, that there was good cause for eating Tansy at Easter time since it purged away the phlegm 'engendered of fish in Lent season'. However tansies are not recommended for present day eating.

St George's Day, 23 April

The origin of George, the patron saint of England, chivalry, cavalrymen and soldiers, is not certain. There are several legends. One says that George was born in the third century and put to death for his Christian faith on 23 April AD 303. He is said to have appeared again to lead the English and Norman forces to victory at Antioch in 1098 and also when Richard I was leading the Crusades against the Saracens. There are also many legends of St George involving conflict with a dragon.

His banner, an upright red cross on a white background, became the flag of England and the red rose its emblem. Edward III founded the Order of the Garter in his name, the noblest of the knightly orders of Europe, with a chapel of St George at Windsor.

It is interesting that William Shakespeare was deemed to have been born on 23 April 1564 and to have died on the same day in 1616.

A symbolic arrangement to commemorate St George could use red roses ordered from a florist because garden roses are not yet available. Some reference to Shakespeare could be incorporated with suitable interpretative accessories, by the side of the flowers.

FORWARD PLANNING

Try glycerining catkins for use later in the year. Use the recipe of one-third glycerine with two-thirds boiling water, stirred together. Place the stem ends into the solution at once, after slitting and scraping the woody stems for about 2 inches (5 cms). The solution should reach at least 2 inches (5 cms) up the stem.

Long, dangling catkins such as those of Garrya elliptica maintain more graceful positions if arranged in Oasis on to which the very hot solution has been poured, instead of being stood upright in a jar.

Houseplants need attention at this time of year so that they will flourish later on. Remove dead leaves, re-pot if necessary, wash off any dust and start giving more water and a liquid feed if they are over six months old.

MAY

May is recognized by the Church as the month of Mary and it is traditionally associated with children and flowers.

Sunny dry days bring on the garden flowers; however all kinds of weather can still be expected, with snow showers possible in Scotland but very rare in the south. Late frosts can be a danger in the garden in some parts of the country. If spring has been late the time is often made up in May, because plants quickly respond to the milder conditions. Summer seems near, with both spring and summer flowers available, and arranging flowers in church becomes less expensive because much garden material is available to stretch shop flowers. There is also plenty of choice. Special flower decorations are often planned for Ascension Day and Whitsunday.

PLANT MATERIAL

Florists' flowers

Many varieties of florists' flowers can be found including spring tulips, irises, anemones and a few narcissi, combined with summer lilies, gerberas, arums, alstroemerias, peonies, sweet peas, gladioli and stocks, which are useful because their rather woody, strong stems are easy to arrange. There are the usual all-the-year carnations, roses and chrysanthemums, and also indoor flowering pot plants of geraniums and pelargoniums, gloxinias, chrysanthemums, fuchsias, hydrangeas, roses and marguerites with the lovely coloured leaves of the annual Coleus blumei, grown for its foliage. The latter needs copious watering which may be difficult to provide regularly in a church. It does not hold up well when cut and is better used as a pot plant.

Gerberas are large daisy-type flowers which show up well and have striking colours of red, orange, yellow, pink and white, but their heads droop quickly if care is not taken in conditioning them.

They are sold with the flowers often shielded in bells of polythene. Before buying make sure that the centres of the flowers are not mouldy and are circular rather than oval, and be certain the heads are not droopy. Unwrap the flowers at home and push them up and out of the

GOOD RESOURCES *Imported 'Green Woodpecker' gladioli with
orange and red tulips and yellow irises in plastic foam. This can be
supported with a cradle of netting overlapped around the vase edge to
which the foam is wired. Or the vase can be filled with sand, pebbles
or old pieces of foam to lift the new foam. Arranged by Rona Coleman.
By courtesy of the Bulb Information Desk.*

106

GOOD RESOURCES *Gerberas in brilliant colours next to a navy cope on the stone steps leading to the Chapter House of Wells Cathedral. The clear perspex stand is hardly noticeable. Arranger Margaret Baker. Photography D. Rendell.*

polythene shield. Cut off half an inch of stem and place them immediately in two inches of water that has just boiled. Leave until the water has cooled and then top up with tepid water. This helps to move water quickly up the stem to prevent the younger part at the top from wilting and it also removes some of the air bubbles that seem to collect in the stems of gerberas. Carry the flowers to church in a jug or bucket of water if possible. They should then last well.

Garden plant material
Until the end of the month it is unwise to use young new leaves, and evergreens are still the standby, except in the south of the country, or in sheltered positions.

Flowering shrubs
In May flowering shrubs are a good source of supply. There are many with long stems for use as outlines, especially in pedestal arrangements.

Shrubs that provide useful branches include azaleas in yellows, oranges, pinks and crimson, but these are slow-growing and it is advisable to cut only from large shrubs. Azaleas should be picked in tight bud because they open quickly. Weigelas, hardy and deciduous, have long arching stems with small pink or crimson flowers. Weigela florida grows six to eight-foot high, and the variety named 'Variegata' has pale pink flowers with green and cream leaves.

Lilac, Syringa vulgaris, is lovely, especially in white or lemon. 'Maud Notcutt', 'Vestale' and 'Candeur' are good white-flowered varieties and 'Primrose' is an attractive yellow. The mauve and purple lilacs do not show up so well in a church. When using them in an arrangement the branches must be defoliated completely; if this is not done, the flowers do not get enough water and quickly wilt.

Broom is a useful shrub for flower arrangers and legend says that it is a magic shrub from which fairies often speak. Cytisus x praecox with cream flowers is a lovely variety to grow. Deutzias have small but numerous white, pink or purple flowers on long arching stems and many rhododendrons are now at their best. Viburnum opulus 'Sterile' (Snowball bush) has large round flower heads that open green and become white in late May and June. The spherical flower provides a good contrast of shape in arrangements. Laburnum and wisteria are very beautiful but unfortunately do not last well when cut.

Allow shrubs to grow to a reasonable size before taking branches for arrangements and cut when the flowers are in bud. It is better to use a sharp knife or secateurs rather than snapping off a branch with the hand because this encourages disease. Cut just above a new bud or where side branches join a main one, so that the shrub grows on.

Remove all or most of the leaves of lilacs, Viburnum opulus and deutzias. Scrape off about 2 inches (5 cms) of the outside bark of the stem end of all branches using a small knife, and slit up the stem end for about the same length. This helps them to take up water. A few inches of boiling or very hot water at first is also helpful.

Flowers

This is a month when peonies can be enjoyed and there is no flower more beautiful for church arrangements. Their large circular flowers are perfect for emphasis in the centre of an arrangement. Two or three flowers are often sufficient when combined with flowering branches or florist's stock or gladioli for height and outline. The double varieties probably last longer when cut.

This is still tulip time and there are lilies-of-the-valley for small arrangements. A German folk story tells that these flowers sprang from Mary's tears shed at the Cross, so they would be an appropriate flower for placing at the foot of a statue of Mary.

Pyrethrums are excellent as cut flowers with varieties in white, through all the pinks, to crimson. Pyrethrum roseum 'Eileen May Robinson' is a lovely pink and P.R. 'Brenda' is deep cerise with 'Avelarde' a good white. They need well-drained soil and a sunny position. They should be cut back after flowering and divided only every 3-4 years.

Poppies appear in late May and Papaver orientale (Oriental Poppy) is the best for cutting. The large flowers can be pink, red or white, usually with a black blotch at the base of the petals. It is important to cut when the bud is just showing colour and to burn the stem ends in a gas jet, match or candle flame. Each time the stem is cut the end should be charred, otherwise the exuding milky fluid clogs the stem end and prevents the uptake of water. Poppies are not long-lasting when cut but are so beautiful and dramatic that they are well worth any extra trouble involved in conditioning and in possible replacement during the week.

Globe Flowers, Trollius x hybridus, are good cut flowers for filling in and their brilliant yellow or orange colouring shows up well. Their stems are around 2 feet (70 cms) long. They need moist soil in sun or partial shade and should be cut back after flowering to induce a second flush of blooms in later summer.

This is the time when it is easy to cut a colourful mixed bunch of flowers from the garden and an arrangement resembling a Flemish or Dutch seventeenth- or eighteenth-century flower painting can give great pleasure (see cover). It is advisable to use a large urn for water, with crumpled wire netting, or a large block of Oasis, because the flowers need plenty of water. Place a tall stemmed, bold flower such as a lily, or a typical Fritillaria imperialis (Crown Imperial), at the top. Florists' flowers, if they can be bought in ones and twos instead of bunches, can make the garden flowers go further.

AVERAGE RESOURCES *Two bunches of cream stock with three pink garden peonies in an alabaster vase using mechanics or foam with a cap of wire netting wired to the vase neck. Crumpled wire netting could be used and ivy or mature hosta leaves can hide the mechanics. Arranger Jean Taylor. Photography D. Rendell.*

Bulb flowers

The spring-flowering bulb flowers have been mentioned already, but in May there are also the useful alliums. They are easy to grow and produce fine spherical flowers in May to June which show up well in church. Allium rosenbachianum has big heads of purple lilac on stems 3 feet (105 cms) tall, flowering in late May. A. aflatunense grows to two and a half feet (76 cms) with 3 inch (7.5 cms) wide umbels. A. giganteum grows to four feet (122 cms) with 4 inch (10 cms) umbels, while A. albopilosum has huge heads 6 inches (15 cms) across on short stems which, when dried, can be lengthened with an artificial stem for use in winter.

Fox-tail Lilies are spectacular garden flowers suitable for church arrangements because of their long-lasting majestic spikes of small flowers in yellow, pink and white. Eremurus bungeri has 2 foot (70 cms) stems and E. himalaicus is similar with white flowers. E. 'Shelford Hybrids' in colours ranging from pale pink to copper orange appear later in June and July.

Wild plant material

New foliage, with the exception of the invaluable bronze-coloured young sycamore, is still immature in May and it wilts quickly, but larch is lovely to use. The graceful branches are a vivid green in March but the needle-like leaves then droop quickly. In May they should last longer and make excellent outlines for flower arrangements, as do branches of wych elm and English elm with their papery green fruits.

Cherry blossom may still be found and there are the pink-tinged buds of wild crab apple. Hawthorn or May-tree is plentiful in the hedgerows, but the flowers only last a day or two. Some say Christ wore a crown of hawthorn and in earlier days in this country it signified the end of winter, the coming of spring and the rebirth of life.

There are many small colourful wild flowers to be found just now, but they will only last a day or two. However these 'flowers of the field' give great pleasure. It is helpful to take a bucket of water or a large polythene bag in the car when gathering them. Place them immediately in water or in the bag, which should be tied at the open end to retain all moisture. Keep the flowers out of sunshine or heat.

Children love to pick bluebells but do warn them that treading on the leaves harms the plant. The early purple orchid is common in the south, often growing with bluebells in woods and grassy places. There are also buttercups and the larger kingcups or marsh-marigolds, Caltha palustris, which grow in wet places. The tiny speedwell is a brilliant blue and there are cuckoo flowers or milkmaids as they are sometimes called. Cowslips grow on banks and in meadows and are plentiful in some places, and the bird's-eye primroses with small pink flowers appear abundantly in Yorkshire and Cumbria in damp, grassy places on peaty soil.

None of these flowers are big or spectacular enough for the main flower arrangements in the church, but they can make a charming small grouping in such places as the children's corner or at the foot of a statue of the Madonna. They are not suitable for Oasis and should be arranged in deep water. Crumpled 2 inch (5 cms) mesh wire netting can be used to support the stems in a bowl. The mesh can be held in place with a rubber band.

Taller wild flowers in May include Queen Anne's Lace, Anthriscus sylvestris (sometimes called Cow Parsley), which whitens many verges so daintily throughout the British Isles from April to June. It provides material for economical arrangements, especially in country churches. There is also the brilliant yellow gorse which, although not long-lasting and impossible to cut without wearing thick gardening gloves, can be seen easily from a distance. The flowers of wild broom, which grows profusely in Scotland, will last a few days in water but the leafy branches are useful for many months of the year. They can be curved with pressure from the warmth of the hand to make gracefully arched stems for outlines.

ALTAR FLOWERS

The cross is the most significant symbol on or near the altar and flowers should enhance or direct attention to it as a dominant feature (see April). However in certain circumstances and with the permission of the clergy, it may be possible to place flowers around it without any way diminishing its importance.

A hidden container of mechanics can be placed behind the cross for supporting the flower stems and providing water. Flowers should be arranged to face different directions to add interest, and a simple arrangement of a few flowers and leaves will not overwhelm the cross.

LIMITED RESOURCES

Country
Queen Anne's lace can be massed in bunches for a country church, but to show up from a distance it is usually necessary to place the flowers close together and to have a dark background. To make bunches tie a length of wool or thread (wire cuts too easily) near the top of a few

GOOD RESOURCES – CITY *Flowers of Lilium longiflorum placed to face in different directions without hiding the cross. Arranged by Mary Graves in the Queen's Chapel of the Savoy. Photography Dennis Barnard*

LIMITED RESOURCES – COUNTRY *Queen Anne's lace tied in tiered bunches. Arranger Jean Taylor. Photography D. Rendell.*

LIMITED RESOURCES – CITY *Florists' carnations and roses with garden privet, ivy and euonymous foliage. More leaves and less flowers could be used for greater economy. Arranger Earlsdon Flower Club members. Photography John Wright.*

grouped stems and then wind it down the stems, tying it again at the bottom. Cut the stems of each bunch to different lengths before tying up each bunch separately. They can then be arranged in a column graduating downwards, the tallest flower stems at the back.

Flowers with a more solid form such as garden pyrethrums or florists' single chrysanthemums can be added if resources allow.

City

There is better value for money when flower arrangements are placed in a high position, such as on a ledge, screen or wall-hook, where they can be seen easily. Start with foliage from a florist or a city garden and then add a few florists' flowers according to available money. When placed in a niche fewer flowers are needed at the back and the sides of the arrangement. When arranged close to a bust or statue, avoid hiding it by placing the flowers to one side or underneath.

IDEA OF THE MONTH

This is a good time to introduce children in the congregation (of ages about eight years upwards, both girls and boys) to flower arranging. School Mayday celebrations should have stimulated an interest in flowers which can be followed up and encouraged. Also flowers are more plentiful for them to pick and arrange at this time.

Formerly children's corners in many churches were decorated with flowers, but sadly this practice has been discontinued in some places. Where it has been maintained it becomes an excellent way of introducing children to arranging church flowers so that, in adult life, they can happily take it up again.

A few classes could be given by a member of the church flower guild (or a teacher from a local flower club) who is used to working with children, meeting at the church or in a home for an hour at weekends. Little expense need be incurred because simplicity is the secret of stimulating interest at first.

A narrow necked container is easy to use in the beginning because mechanics are not necessary. Children can then be taught how to crumple wire netting and place it in a small but deep bowl, using a rubber band to hold it in place. They can then be shown how to conceal the netting with plain flat leaves such as those of ivies, geraniums, small bergenias and honesty or with sprigs of yew or box, finally adding a few flowers. The only guidelines necessary for the positioning of flowers are that each flower should be clearly seen and not put too near to another one. It should be pointed out that flowers look more interesting when turned to face in different directions so

116

that the backs and sides may be seen as well as the fronts. It can also be demonstrated that if stems are cut to different lengths the flowers appear at different heights, some standing tall and others tucked in to avoid a flat look; this helps each flower to be seen. When money is available Oasis can be used in a container especially made to hold a round block firmly in position.

Colour is something that could be left to personal choice at first, although different colour combinations should be shown to increase awareness of colour. The children could also be introduced to texture

A narrow-necked vase for a few flowers

 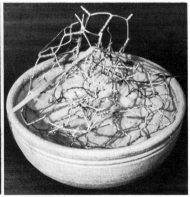

A small bowl of children's flowers   The mechanics

and shown how contrasting textures look more interesting than similar ones. Plant material could be grouped into 'rough-looking' and 'smooth-looking'. An appreciation of curving stems and how they should be placed will be of lasting value as will an awareness of space and how it is used in an arrangement.

Scale is an important aspect and a child soon observes that in an arrangement flowers and leaves should be in scale with each other as well as with the container. This can be shown by comparing the relative sizes of a tiny leaf and a big flower with a correctly scaled leaf and flower. In the same way, scale can be demonstrated with containers and plant material of varying sizes.

The position of the flowers in the church can be discussed and how they should complement the church furnishings. There can also be lessons on flowers for various special occasions, and on the legends of flowers.

Children should be introduced to pinholders, if enough can be borrowed. Each child can bring a low baking dish and some Plasticine from home and be taught how to secure a pinholder in a dish. A few branches from the garden or countryside can then be impaled, emphasizing the need for care because of the sharp pins. Two or three flowers can be added in the space between the twigs, with leaves to cover the pinholder, or the children may enjoy finding stones to conceal the pinholder.

It is important that each child is assigned a Saturday on which to arrange the flowers for Sunday services. This can be done through the parish magazine or by a roster on the church noticeboard. Whoever is responsible for the children's work should give some help the first time. It may be difficult to stand back and allow the child to arrange the

Twigs and flowers in a baking dish. Photography D. Rendell.

flowers alone, but this is important if the child is to feel the work is his or her own. Perfection is not so important as stimulatng enthusiasm to learn and participate.

A junior flower club may be in existence locally. Alternatively more sophisticated lessons may be gradually undertaken and ideas will also come from the children.

SPECIAL OCCASION FLOWERS

GOOD RESOURCES *The font in St Paul's Cathedral decorated for the NAFAS Festival of Flowers, with foxtail lilies in the centre. By courtesy of The Flower Arranger.*

A font makes a suitable container for flowers because of its shape. However it is debatable whether one should be used for this purpose and permission should always be asked to use it. For a special occasion it often provides a position for a flower decoration away from the front of the church.

Pink and white dahlias, carnations and single chrysanthemums for the base of the font in the Church of St Mary, Warwick.
In May peonies could be substituted for the dahlias.
Arranger Anne Horseley. Photography John Wright.

The cavity of the font is usually too large for a container and needs to be reduced in some way. A smaller bowl can be placed inside for mechanics but this may need to be raised from beneath by means of an upturned bowl or a block of wood. It is better to try different methods for the particular font to be decorated because they all differ slightly in shape. One way is to get a wooden board made to fit over the cavity; the bowl for flowers can then be placed on top of it. If there is a likelihood of a christening this is a good method because the flowers and the board can be moved easily.

The arrangement should be tall to balance the visual weight of the font and rarely do arrangements appear sufficiently large. Both flowers and foliage should be big or long-stemmed for good proportion. If the font is visualized in the same way as a smaller container, then it is easy to imagine the height of arrangement necessary.

When the font itself cannot be used, an arrangement can be placed at the base instead.

FLOWERS AND FOLIAGE FOR FESTIVALS AND SAINT DAYS

May Day, 1 May
Originally there was a pagan festival on May Day, but later it came to have religious associations. In medieval and Tudor England it was a great public holiday when villagers processed, carrying green boughs of sycamore and hawthorn, and a tall young tree decorated with garlands of flowers and ribbons. The flowers were often made into crowns, floral spheres, cowslip balls and intertwined garlands, like a Christmas kissing bough, while the tree itself eventually became the maypole. Recently there has been a revived interest in this, with children's dances and the plaiting of brightly coloured ribbons into patterns around the maypole.

May Day which in the Church's year is celebrated as the Feast of Saint Philip and Saint James, has become the children's day, with processions often accompanied by the crowning of a May Queen. Local customs are many and varied and can be followed through, if desired, in church decorations, especially for weddings or other special occasions.

A 'maypole' decoration
This can be made in a formal manner like a clipped topiary tree or informally with the appearance of a flower arrangement on top of a long stem. The basic constructions to support the plant material is the same.

Method Hammer a 2 inch (5 cms) flat-headed nail into the top of a broom handle, that has been painted dark brown or green, or a broad bamboo cane. Saw off the end to the desired length, allowing about 4 inches (10 cms) to go into the pot and about 1 inch (2.5 cms) for the arrangement on the top. Tall or short-stemmed trees can be made but for stability, the taller ones must be weighted at the bottom, or tied to something at the top, otherwise they are easily blown or knocked over.

Secure the lower end of the stem using plaster of Paris, in a bowl or plant pot made of plastic to avoid cracking. Fill the bowl with the powder (obtainable in bags from a chemist) and stir in cold water until it is a thick paste. Insert the stem end at once, making certain it is vertical. Hold it in position for a minute or two until the plaster is set.

Place the plastic bowl inside a more decorative container or a pleasing plant pot and cover the plaster with gravel, pebbles or shattered windscreen glass. Impale a half block of soaked Oasis on to the nail, pressing down until the top of the stem enters the foam. If the arrangement is to last for several days it may be advisable to wrap the foam in thin polythene to conserve moisture. Cover the foam with foliage before adding flowers. The looser, taller-stemmed style needs

A formal tree. Arranger Jean Taylor. Photography D. Rendell.

An informal variation. Arranger Jean Taylor. Photography D. Rendell.

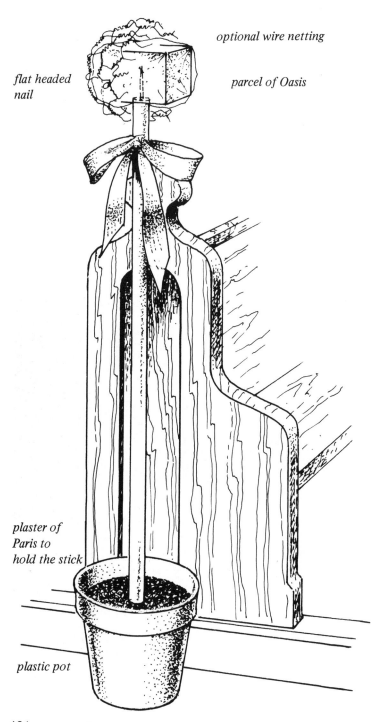

optional wire netting

flat headed
nail

parcel of Oasis

plaster of
Paris to
hold the stick

plastic pot

trailing leaves to soften the appearance. A bow of ribbon can be added for suitable occasions.

When several such trees are made for Christmas or a wedding they can be prepared ahead of time and the flowers added just before the occasion. Box with woody stems (obtainable from a flower shop) will last for weeks if, after it is arranged, the whole sphere is wrapped in thin polythene or a polythene bag. (See also *Flowers in Church* page 130).

Rogation Days

The name comes from the Latin 'rogare' meaning to beseech or ask for. Rogation Sunday, which may fall in April, is the fifth after Easter and the three days following it are Rogation Days when in earlier times processions were led through the cornfields and prayers were made for the growing crops and the coming harvest. In a modern version of this ceremony at St Clement Danes in London, and in other churches, the

'Ascension', interpretations by Joy Gray and Lynn Simms. By courtesy of The Flower Arranger.

125

processions include schoolboys carrying willow wands topped with ribbons or wild flowers.

Ascension Day

Ascension Day, known as Holy Thursday in old English usage, is the fortieth day after Easter and is one of the great festivals of the Christian year. It has been observed probably since the fourth century.

The earliest celebration seems to have originated in Jerusalem to commemorate the journey made by the apostles from Jerusalem to Bethany and the Mount of Olives. In Western churches the paschal candle is extinguished to signify Christ's departure from the apostles and it now commemorates the ascension into heaven, forty days after his resurrection.

Flower arrangements to signify this day could be tall and uplifting, such as gladioli or fox-tail lilies arranged vertically; an experienced flower arranger could make an interpretative arrangement. White is the symbolic colour used by the Church.

Pentecost and Whit Sunday

The Christian season of Pentecost or Whitsuntide, seven weeks or fifty days after Easter, corresponds to the Jewish festival of Weeks, or Pentecost, in the same way that the Christian Easter corresponds to Passover. At Pentecost the Holy Spirit came to the disciples in tongues of fire, giving them power to go into the world to tell of their belief. Because of the fire, red is the colour used for Pentecost and red gladioli or roses can be used in arrangements.

Whit Sunday can fall in May or June and is the seventh Sunday after Easter. Originally it is thought to have been 'White Sunday' when, in an ancient custom, white robes were worn by the newly baptized at the feast of Pentecost, a special time for both baptism and confirmation.

It could be significant to have an arrangement of white flowers on or near the font. Among old customs in some countries on this day were the blowing of trumpets, throwing down of burning torches from the roof (not to be advised), the releasing of doves in the church and the scattering of roses. In England during the Middle Ages money was traditionally contributed for upkeep of the church buildings, and parish churches sold Church or Whitsun Ales, often in the church itself.

FORWARD PLANNING

Planting

Chrysanthemums

These can be planted out ready for autumn cutting. Hundreds of varieties are available and because new ones are introduced each year, it is better to study the current catalogue of a specialist grower before ordering.

There are useful single and double spray chrysanthemums which require no disbudding and grow into natural sprays. If planted in May or June they flower in August to October ready for harvest festivals. Other useful outdoor chrysanthemums are the blooms which have been disbudded for producing a large flower. They can be cut from August to September if planted in May and June.

Pompons are normally too small for church flower arrangements and the varieties with long thin quilled petals grown under glass are very beautiful but rather too delicate in form to show up from a distance. When a cool greenhouse or conservatory is available collections can be bought for planting in May to July for cutting from October until Christmas. Large single chrysanthemums, obtained by disbudding, are especially dramatic.

Dahlias

Rooted cuttings and sprouted tubers of dahlias can be planted out during the third week in May, if it is not cold and wet. The most useful are the larger varieties which provide a big bright flower for church arrangements, but any dahlias provide good cut flowers. It is again a matter of choice from the many varieties and a visit to a local garden centre or grower is advisable. The water-lily dahlias are lovely with beautiful colourings. Bigger flowers result from allowing only one flower to a stem, removing all side buds and shoots at an early stage. They will flower from early August until the frosts begin.

Seedheads

Lunaria annua (honesty) has an excellent seedhead for use in winter. The silver papery moon shapes last indefinitely and so some flowers should be left in the ground to go to seed for cutting and also for supplying future flowers, because this plant is a biennial.

JUNE

June is usually a warm, fine month with a profusion of flowers in the garden which continues until September. The scent of flowers, with a stillness in the air, makes this a beautiful time in the British year. It is a favourite month for weddings, to keep the church flower arranger busy, but the taller and larger flowers and leaves of summer make big arrangements quick and easy to accomplish.

Young, deciduous foliage is sufficiently mature by now to last well in water, and slower-growing evergreens can be left uncut to grow on for winter use. Choice is plentiful in both gardens and flower shops; the only problem may be one of selection.

This is the time to experiment with unusual colour schemes and combinations of flowers and foliage and spectacular arrangements can be made cheaply. The light summer evenings, picnics in the countryside and holidays provide opportunities for gathering useful wild plant material wherever it grows in profusion.

PLANT MATERIAL

Florists' flowers
The florist trade is well into the summer crops which arrive in abundance in June. There are good buys in delphiniums, stocks, sweet Williams, alstroemerias, antirrhinums, sweet peas and lilies. Tulips, lilies-of-the-valley and irises are still obtainable and supplies of gladioli are increasing. Scabious starts its long season and there are even a few early dahlias.

Some flower shops sell tall spikes of eremurus with their small, star-shaped flowers in orange shades. They can be combined with the blue or white large globular flowers of agapanthus, the African Lily, to make dramatic large designs which last well.

Garden plant material
There are so many flowers at this time of the year that a full list would be lengthy. Many varieties are grown, according to personal preference and local conditions.

Especially useful for church arrangements at this time are the flowers of roses, hostas, delphiniums, lupins, larkspurs, monkshoods, peonies, alliums, campanulas, irises, the late lilacs and the green flower heads of angelica. Lady's Mantle (Alchemilla mollis) has only a small flower but it is such a brilliant lime green that it shows up well and also seems to enhance other colours. It can be massed to good effect. The round leaves are as useful as geranium leaves for concealing mechanics. The

AVERAGE RESOURCES *Small flowers from a garden massed in a candlestick with a candlecup. Lady's Mantle is seen lower left and the colours are pinks, reds and green with roses used for central emphasis. Arranger Bill Lomas, photography D. Rendell.*

130

asiatic flowering dogwood with white bracts (Cornus kousa chinensis) is very beautiful, but laburnum, so spectacular in the garden, does not last when cut, even when defoliated and sprayed. Choisya with its glossy, dark, evergreen leaves carries star-like white flowers in May and June, and Euphorbia characias 3'-4' tall has evergreen leaves in mild winters and spectacular green bracts.

The leaves of hostas, in many sizes and shades of green, are invaluable at this time of year. If you are without a supply do plant some as soon as possible because they are easily grown and can be used from May until October. They are most adaptable; the leaves can be used with long or short stems, in traditional or modern designs, as a background for flowers, as fillers, as graceful shapes arranged alone and to hide mechanics.

Trails of leaves are useful for softening the appearance of pedestal containers; for these use periwinkles, honeysuckles, the new growth of ivies and Yellow Archangel (Lamium galeobdolon 'Variegata') which is an excellent, though rampant, ground cover with silver-flushed leaves.

Whatever flowers and leaves you cut from the vast choice in June it is important to condition them well and, once placed in an arrangement, to spray them often with a light mist of water. Apart from grey foliage, leaves can be conditioned by submerging or floating them in cool water for about two hours. This cuts down transpiration and the leaves become turgid through their water content. On the other hand, if grey foliage is soaked the tiny hairs – which give the grey effect – become waterlogged; the result is loss of greyness and a dripping leaf. Once soaked, leaves can be put in a polythene bag with the open end tied up. They will remain turgid for a day or two without further soaking.

Conditioning and arranging some popular June flowers

Roses

Roses, gracing almost every garden in June, are a joy to behold. Bigger blooms, suitable for church arrangements, can be obtained by disbudding at an early stage. They are ideal for arrangement because they can be used alone with their own excellent foliage, but also combine well with other flowers. The bud is a lovely shape and as it opens it provides a good transitional form. The wide open flowers are excellent for emphasis in a design, especially for the centre of a traditional arrangement. Long sprays of shrub roses, picked when the flowers are in bud, are ideal for the outlines of arrangements. Roses do not last for more than two or three days unless conditioned well. The following steps are helpful:

1 Pick when the flower is in bud but showing colour.
2 Remove lower leaves and thorns and slit up the stem end for about 1 inch to help water absorption.
3 Stand the stem ends in water that has just boiled. This helps the top, young part of the stem to take in water more rapidly. When the water cools fill up the jug or bucket with tepid water.
4 Leave the container of roses in a cool, dim place away from heat or strong sunlight until ready to make an arrangement. A large polythene bag placed over the roses will help to conserve moisture.
5 Preferably carry the roses to the church in the covered container of water or, if this is not practical, place the roses in the bag and tie up the end.
6 Arrange the stems in deep water rather than Oasis if there is a choice.
7 Spray the flowers, especially large ones, with water before leaving the church and again, if possible, each following day.
8 If a rose wilts remove it from the arrangement and float it in tepid water for about two hours to revive it.

It is possible to have roses for a special occasion up till Christmas. Pick them in bud and dip the stem ends in melted candle wax (use the wax as soon as it is melted and watch that it does not become too hot and burst into flames). Lay the roses in a cardboard box stored in a cool place. When the flowers are to be used, cut off the waxed ends and place the stems in warm water.

Peonies

These lovely flowers are easy to arrange because they have strong stems. The stem does not wilt but the petals, because there are so many, can become soft and floppy. Spraying the flower with water is helpful.

Peonies in bud, but showing colour, can be kept for a special occasion by leaving them without water in a very cool room, preferably on a stone or tiled floor. If they are to be left for more than a day or two, tie them up in a plastic bag. This treatment retards development which resumes at normal pace when the stems are recut and placed in warm water.

The leaves of peonies do not last as long as the flowers; other foliage, such as Hosta, is a better complement.

Delphiniums and lupins

These flowers look the most effective when arranged alone with a few leaves from other plants. Both are tall and stately for church arrangements. Lupins come in many colours and colour combinations, and delphiniums can be grown in an array of blues and violets, pinks, white and yellow. The violets and darker blues are not as effective in church as the lighter colours.

It is important to pick them when young. If there is any possibility of falling petals, give them a good shake before placing them in an arrangement, but usually they are past their best at this stage. Conditioning is also important; the hollow stems can be filled with water by means of a small watering can with a narrow spout. When full, place your thumb over the end of the stem and immediately put it into a bucket of water. Alternatively it can be plugged with cotton wool or Oasis which helps to hold in the water. Each time a stem is cut it should be cut under water and refilled.

Foxgloves

Many people allow foxgloves to seed themselves freely in the garden and the mauve and white varieties are common in the wild. They are best treated as biennials but are well worth cultivating because they are useful when fresh as a tall spiky flower and also, in winter, as a glycerined seedhead.

Digitalis purpurea 'Sutton's Apricot' with a 5-foot stem is beautiful for church arrangements and especially for weddings in June and July. The 'Excelsior', 5-foot tall, and the shorter 'Foxy' strain are excellent for cutting. D. grandiflora has yellow flowers a little later on.

Just as with delphiniums and lupins, foxgloves can look spectacular when arranged with bold foliage but without other flowers. They are also useful for giving height to an arrangement of mixed flowers. They lose dignity when cut with short stems.

Pick in bud and stand in tepid water for a few hours before arranging the flowers. Spray the top of the stem with water sometimes.

The new flower arranger

This is a good time of the year for the newer flower arranger to practise because there are plenty of flowers and leaves at little or no cost. Oasis is the easiest stem support to use because the stems stay exactly where they are placed and angles can be used which are not possible with a pinholder or wire netting. But it is a good idea to practise with wire netting because it is less expensive than Oasis. Also, many experts think that summer flowers last better in hot weather if they are put in deep water with the stems supported by wire netting. *(See Flowers in Church* by Jean Taylor, Chapter 2).

There are no rules and you can begin an arrangement wherever you wish. Many arrangers establish the height first. As a rough guide the tallest stem can be two-and-a-half to three times the height of the container, but this depends on the visual weight of the container. Some surfaces and materials attract more attention than others and the stems should be taller to offset this and give pleasing proportions. Sometimes the longest stem finishes up looking too tall, but if necessary this can be shortened before the arrangement is finished.

Step 1 Place well-soaked Oasis in a deep container, such as an urn, with the foam standing two or three inches above the container's rim. Position tall stems of such flowers as foxgloves, lupins, delphiniums or monkshoods for height. Then add leaves of hostas, laurel, Lady's Mantle, geraniums or bergenias, with stems of different lengths; they add another shape, conceal the foam and provide a plain background for flowers.

Step 1   *Step 2*

134

Step 2 For central emphasis add round flowers, such as peonies, daisy-type flowers or open roses. They can be used with stems of varying

Step 3 Arranger Jean Taylor, photography D. Rendell

length in a vertical line, but a straight line is not normally as attractive as a curved one. Larger flowers should be centrally placed in this style with smaller ones at the top and bottom. If all the flowers are the same size, turn some flower heads on their sides to make them look smaller.

Step 3 Fill in the sides with a few more sprays of flowers and leaves to make the arrangement wider. The final shape can be compact, or more space can be left within the design, according to choice.

Wild plant material

Lords-and-Ladies (Arum maculatum) can be discovered growing in damp places such as ditches; it has a useful plain leaf. Bronze, young leaves of sycamores can still be found and for a dainty, pretty leaf there is Wild Carrot (Daucus carota). The flowers of hogweed or cow parsnip (Heracleum sphondylium) are a dainty green 'filler' for summer arrangements. The whitebeam tree (Sorbus aria) has clean-looking leaves with white undersides and is in flower in May and June. Reedmace, commonly called bulrush, can be cut with long stems and arranged alone at floor level in stately designs or used for height in arrangements of mixed flowers. Pennywort (Umbilicus rupestris), which grows in the south, has wands of yellow-green for smaller arrangements.

The many wild flowers out at this time include trails of varieties of dog rose, yellow irises growing in wet places, curls of wild honeysuckle, tall purple loosestrife, willowherb and foxglove, all of which are pink-mauve and last a few days if picked in bud. Horsechestnut flowers in white or red are stately in May and June, and when cut with long curving stems they can make spectacular large arrangements. It is advisable to defoliate the stems so that the available water reaches the flowers. Rhododendron ponticum, the wild rhododendron, grows in abundance on acid soils and should be picked also in the bud stage. Field poppies, so tempting because of their brilliant colour, do not last well when cut and look their best when wind-blown in the meadows.

The Guelder Rose (Viburnum opulus) with its creamy flower is very pretty but does not last well, although it does help if the stem is defoliated in the same way as elder and Mountain Ash, or rowan, which is common everywhere. This was a significant tree in pre-Christian religions because it was used to protect men from evil.

In small arrangements nothing can look prettier in a country church than Ox-eye Daisy (Leucanthemum vulgare), also called marguerite or Dog Daisy. It grows in abundance in many places and can look charming with the common Red Campion (Silene dioica). False Oxlip, a hybrid between cowslip and primrose, occurs where both grow together; it is a fresh yellow flower useful for small arrangements.

136

It is important to place wild flowers out of heat and sunshine as soon as they are cut. A bucket of water or a polythene bag in the car is helpful. Once home, recut the stem ends and put them in an inch of boiling water for a few minutes before placing them in a bucket of tepid water covered with a polythene bag, in a cool dark place to reduce transpiration. It is helpful to float wild flowers on cool water. They should be arranged in church as soon as possible after conditioning.

ALTAR FLOWERS

White flowers show up well on an altar or communion table, especially when against a dark background. There are many white flowers in June, including roses, delphiniums, foxgloves, lilies, lilacs, gladioli, carnations, campanulas, larkspurs and spray chrysanthemums. Many people like white flowers for altar arrangements, especially for weddings and other special occasions.

Mock Orange (Philadelphus) has sweet-scented white flowers which do not last long, but are so delightful that they are worth arranging just for a short time. They last better if most of the leaves are cut off the stem, because these take away water from the flowers. Some trimming may be necessary because the branches can grow at unattractive angles. The stems make a pretty outline for white lilies used in the centre of an arrangement, with leaves of hosta, geraniums or Alchemilla mollis to conceal the mechanics and soften the bare appearance of the woody branches.

The familiar brass altar vase can overwhelm dainty white flowers in colour and brilliance. For a change, an alabaster urn can look beautiful, but because the material is porous it is advisable to line the cavity with a plastic or tin container to hold mechanics and water.

LIMITED RESOURCES

Country
Green always looks lovely in a country church, especially if several shades of green are used in one arrangement. It is also more interesting to see a variety of shapes. Angelica archangelica, often called Holy Ghost, is a spectacular plant in the garden at this time of year, growing up to 7-feet tall. The rounded flowers are followed by seedheads which vary in size from 6-12 inches in diameter.

The foliage wilts quickly and is better discarded. Instead use the leaves of irises, hostas and ivies for a change of greens and to soften the look of the bare stems. Young flowers are inclined to wilt so it is better to cut them when mature or in the early seed stage and to use deep water for the stems.

AVERAGE RESOURCES *Mock orange branches with white lilies and leaves of hosta and Alchemilla mollis arranged by Jean Taylor, photography D. Rendell.*

LIMITED RESOURCES – COUNTRY *Angelica heads combined with foliage of hosta, irises and ivies in an 18-inch tall green-black hand-made urn. Arranger Jean Taylor, photography D. Rendell.*

City

Sweet William in colourful bunches can be found in florists' shops at low cost. Used singly, the flowers may lose their impact, but when massed in shades of pinks and reds they provide a wealth of colour. Arranged in a simple earthenware jug with a few leaves at the base, they make an informal small arrangement.

LIMITED RESOURCES – CITY *Sweet William bunched in a simple jug by Jean Taylor. Photography D. Rendell.*

A few city garden roses, or six from a florist, can add colour to a pot-et-fleur which is on permanent display in a city church.

LIMITED RESOURCES – CITY *A pot-et-fleur arranged by Mrs M. Ridgway. By courtesy of The Flower Arranger. Photography D. Rendell.*

GOOD RESOURCES *'The Royal Company of Archers' featured with an all green arrangement by Mrs Trudy McEwan. Photography D. Rendell. By courtesy of The Flower Arranger.*

Interpretative arrangements

Flowers in church are normally arranged to make a more beautiful setting for the acts of worship, to bring life and colour into the building and to inspire worship through the appreciation of nature.

In more recent years flower festivals, arranged by church flower guilds or flower arrangement clubs affiliated to the National Association of Flower Arrangement Societies of Great Britain, or both groups working together, have introduced interpretative arrangements for church congregations and visitors. These have stimulated great interest

LIMITED RESOURCES *'St Helen's Hospice, Bishopsgate', an interpretative arrangement by Mrs B. Glover. Photography Fox-Waterman. By courtesy of The Flower Arranger.*

and have communicated thoughts and knowledge to people in the same way that medieval Renaissance painters communicated legends and meanings through the symbolic flowers in their pictures.

These interpretative arrangements are inappropriate on or near the altar, and should not be used as a main church flower arrangement. However, at the back of the church an interpretative arrangement could excite interest and stimulate thought at a regular church service, in the same way as at the special, but only occasional, flower festivals.

AVERAGE RESOURCES *'A Christmas Canticle' arranged by Mrs M. Guerson. Photography James A. Fennemore Associates.*

Interpretative arrangements should be left usually to more experi-ended flower arrangers who have had some practice at 'communicating' through plant material at flower shows. The church is not an appropriate place for many accessories, drapes, backgrounds and bases, and sim-plicity should normally be the rule and is often the most effective method of communication. Often the plant material itself can convey

GOOD RESOURCES *'St Joan of Arc – The Warrior' arranged in the Collegiate Church of St Mary, Warwick, by Mrs Joyce Clements. Photography John Wright. By courtesy of The Flower Arranger.*

meaning without additional objects, but sometimes dignified and simple accessories and a well-written card can be added to help convey the message.

A great variety of themes are possible including texts, passages from the Bible, local history, the Church Calendar, tributes to Saints and famous people, special national or local events, charities and so on. Some preliminary discussion at the flower guild's meetings is advisable to help the development of ideas.

SPECIAL OCCASION FLOWERS

Arrangements of one type of flower have been neglected in recent years in favour of mixed flowers and leaves with many colours and textures. But featuring one type of flower can be most effective. It emphasizes the shape, colour, texture and character of the flower and makes a strong impact on the viewer.

Before making the arrangement, think about the particular flower's habit of growth and its special qualities. Delphiniums, for example, are dignified flowers which look their best with the stems at full length in vertical designs. Gladioli look like leaping flames and their shape suits a fan-shaped design. Lilies-of-the-valley are dainty and suitable for massing on or near a font, when available in quantity. Daisy flowers usually look their best arranged informally in baskets and jugs.

Not every type of flower is suitable to arrange on its own. Circular flowers such as dahlias, for example, may give a static appearance unless the flowers are turned and used with leaves or flowers of other plants. However, it is worth giving thought to this idea when considering a church arrangement, especially for a festival or special occasion when so often the eyes can tire of mixed groups.

FLOWERS AND FOLIAGE FOR FESTIVALS AND SAINT DAYS

June 10, St Margaret of Scotland

St Margaret brought up a family of eight, one of whom became the re-nowned Queen Maud of England, Margaret's brother being Saxon heir to the English throne. Her piety and concern for the poor was famous throughout the known world. An arrangement using simple plant material from the countryside could interpret her life. She is now the patron saint of women, nurses and peasants.

June 24, St John the Baptist

St John was born six months before Christ. He went into retirement in the wilderness, becoming an anchorite, and after 30 years emerged to fulfil Isaiah's prophecy that there would be someone to prepare the way for Jesus. He gathered many followers through his pure life and

AVERAGE RESOURCES *Fans of gladioli in flame colours interpreting 'Now the year is crowned with blessing', arranged by Bill Lomas around the altar for a festival All Saints Parish Church, Daresbury. Photography D. Rendell.*

AVERAGE RESOURCES *Lilies-of-the-valley arranged by Mrs Angela Whitcombe in St Peter's Church, Seaview, Isle of Wight, for a festival. The flowers kept fresh for four days and were arranged in small containers of Oasis on a fitted board.*

words which preached against the worldliness of life in his time. Jesus was baptized in the wilderness by him and some time after this John was imprisoned and beheaded for political reasons.

The most complete account of his life can be read in the Gospel according to St Luke. His life in the wildnerness could be interpreted with a simple arrangement of driftwood and cactus.

June 29, St Peter and St Paul

This is the feast of two of Christ's Apostles. Peter was a fisherman, a man of great simplicity, courage and sincerity who could be outspoken at times and rash in action. He is now the patron saint of bakers, butchers and clockmakers.

Paul was a Christian missionary and theologian and is now considered by many to have been the greatest apostle of Christianity. He is the patron saint of musicians. His journeys could be interpreted, or flowers with accessories could reflect the groups of which both men are now the patron saints.

FORWARD PLANNING

Drying and preserving plant material for winter use begins to be a major activity at this time.

Drying

Grasses should be dried when young because they then retain their colour. Cut them as soon as they emerge and hang them up in small bunches in a dry place. Bulrushes, if cut before pollination, will remain intact and not explode in several weeks' time scattering their fluffy seeds far and wide. However, if need be, explosion can be prevented by spraying the bulrush with hair lacquer or clear varnish. Broom wands can be tied with string into circles and dried in a warm place.

Alliums can be hung to dry but the heads should hang free without touching anything in order to retain the globular shape. A hook in the ceiling or a clothes-drying rack or a rope across a room can be used. Delphiniums and larkspurs dry well. Although larkspurs can be dried in bunches, delphiniums are better dried singly to avoid crushing the flowers. They retain their blue colour well, but avoid purple flowers which become almost black, and lavender ones which become grey. Quick drying in a dark place such as the airing cupboard gives the best results in colour retention. A few days is long enough. It is better to pick delphiniums and larkspurs for drying just as the top buds are opening.

PRESERVING

Whitebeam preserves well, with one side of the leaf turning dark brown and the underside pale grey. Foxglove seedheads are especially successful and should be picked when the last flower is at the top of the stem. This can be removed after the treatment. The stems turn a pale brown and are invaluable for height in winter arrangements.

PLANTING

If not already completed, continue to plant geraniums because their round leaves are excellent for concealing mechanics. Half-hardy zinnias, asters, African marigolds, dahlias, tobacco plant (Nicotiana affinis), stocks and the silver-leafed foliage plants of Cineraria maritima and Senecio cineraria should also be planted this month for late summer use.

JULY

July is often the hottest month of the year with the highest temperatures occurring inland in the Home Counties and Fen district; often the coastal areas are cooler, especially in the north and west of the country. If there is a drought, watering the garden is necessary at least twice a week, unless restricted by the authorities. But July can also be the wettest month of summer with heavy downpours and thunderstorms; staking the tall-stemmed flowers used in church arrangements is advisable. Many people go on holiday and the church flower rota needs careful planning. Looking ahead to winter, this is the month to preserve deciduous foliage with glycerine and to glean and dry many flowers and some seedheads.

PLANT MATERIAL

A church is fortunately a cool place in hot weather, where flowers last better than anywhere else. However, the sultry air makes it essential to condition flowers well before arranging them, especially in city churches. Garden flowers are not as reliable as some florists' flowers when there is a heatwave.

If it can be organized a daily spray of tepid water is beneficial to arrangements and is the best way to prevent wilting flowers. Blooms with numerous petals, such as large open roses, should be avoided because they cause greater transpiration, but the daisy-type flowers last well.

Leaves are the best stand-by in a heat wave. They are long-lasting because all foliage is now mature and there are no dropping petals to untidy the church. Greens are cool to look at and can be very refreshing on a hot day.

Florists' flowers

At this time of the year florists buy their flowers and plants from many sources including nurseries, markets and private gardens. This gives a wide selection for the arranger who is prepared to shop around.

Basic stocks include lilies in several colours, sweet peas, carnations, roses, dahlias, long-lasting alstroemerias in several colours, asters, stocks and spray chrysanthemums, including white 'Bonnie Jean', a single

AVERAGE RESOURCES *A long-lasting, cool-looking design for hot weather in greens, arranged by Bill Lomas. Included are seed heads of angelica, tall stems of grey-green Scotch Thistle and foliage of irises. hostas, Fatsia japonica, gold splashed elaeagnus and grey-green artichoke. Photographer D. Rendell.*

LIMITED RESOURCES *A simple white and green arrangement of small gladioli and the white chrysanthemum 'Bonnie Jean' with leaves of hosta and periwinkle for a long-lasting cool design in a brass candlestick. A pair could be used for an altar. Arranger Jean Taylor. Photographer D. Rendell.*

daisy-type flower which looks cool in warm weather.

Gladioli are available in an almost unlimited range of colours in shops as well as gardens from July to September. Large-flowered gladioli growing 3-6 feet tall with flowers 4 inches in diameter are magnificent for church arrangements, especially when used without other flowers. Primulinus gladioli have elegant, hooded flowers, many in soft delicate colours on slender stems about 3-feet tall, ideal for smaller arrangements. The flowers are not as regular as the larger-flowered gladioli and the stems have a less stiff appearance. The flowers of butterfly gladioli are a little larger than the primulinus varieties, with attractive colour combinations and ruffled petals. The smaller varieties are found in early and mid-season, but the larger ones can be obtained until late autumn.

Garden plant material
Cutting

In warm weather cut early in the morning or late in the evening. The midday sun in July causes plants to transpire rapidly and many flowers wilt before they are cut. They then take longer to condition and some never recover. In the early morning the stems are turgid after the night hours. In the evening plants are beginning to recover from the effects of the hot sun and recuperate quickly when placed in buckets of deep water overnight in a cool, dim room such as a cellar, washhouse or garage without a draught. They are ready to be arranged the following morning.

If a downpour seems likely cut delicate flowers before it arrives because heavy rain can do considerable damage to flowers, although leaves are not affected and even benefit from a soaking.

In warmer weather be especially careful to cut flowers in bud, just showing colour, because buds open quickly.

Gladioli should be cut when the lower florets are just opening, leaving at least three leaves on the plant so that the young corms for the following year obtain proper nutriment. Remove the top tight buds from the stems because, if this is done, the flowers below should then last longer.

Available flowers and leaves

Gardens can supply lilies in a number of colours, dahlias, antirrhinums, astilbes, stocks, sweet peas, marigolds, zinnias in many brilliant colours, roses, larkspurs, tobacco plant (Nicotiana affinis). There are the useful campanulas which do not drop their petals, including the white form of Campanula persicifolia which lasts well.

Kniphofia (Red Hot Poker) has so many forms that there can be flowers available from June to October. The usual red and orange ones can be cut with stems 3-4 feet long and they are versatile in arrangements. But cream 'Maid of Orleans' and yellow 'Brimstone' flower later and are delightful for smaller arrangements.

There are two sea hollies which are excellent to use at this time of the year and which can be dried or preserved. Eryngium alpinum has large flowers with frothy bracts in steel blue, and although a short-lived perennial in the garden, the flowers last well when cut and are worth planting. Eryngium giganteum, a hardy biennial with blue-grey flowers surrounded by a silvery, prickly collar, grows 3-4 feet tall. Both varieties combine well with many flowers.

AVERAGE RESOURCES *Garden flowers and foliage including orange lilies, yellow kniphofia and yarrow with daisies, ferns and leaves of Alchemilla mollis in a blue-grey Spanish vase, arranged by Jean Taylor. Photographer D. Rendell.*

The flowers of the perennial phlox are good for filling in arrangements of bolder flowers and they can be cut from mid-July through August. Phlox paniculata 'Admiral' is a good white and, amongst many others, there are 'Prince of Orange' and soft pink 'Mother of Pearl'. The flowers must be cut and placed in water immediately because once wilted they do not recover. But, this having been done, they last well. Dead flowers should be cut off and the buds will continue to open.

The Peruvian Lily can be grown in the garden and hybrids of Alstroemeria ligtu are not difficult. The sturdier Peruvian Lilies are found in florists' shops. They provide good 'fillers' on long stems, with pink, cream or orange flowers.

Love-lies-bleeding (Amaranthus caudatus) is invaluable with green or dark red tassel flowers to drip over the rims of containers, especially in pedestal arrangements. Buddleia lasts only two days and must be defoliated if it is to last at all, but Buddleia fallowiana 'Alba' with cream-white flowers is worth growing for wedding arrangements when the flowers need last only a day. Buddleia davidii 'White Cloud' has a profusion of dense flower spikes. The forms with violet flowers are of little use in church because the colour recedes.

There is no shortage of foliage, including the invaluable hostas, Sedum x 'Autumn Joy' and the grey Lamb's Ear (Stachys lanata). Leaves with a thick outer covering last longer in warm weather than thinner leaves which soon wilt from lack of moisture.

Tall plant material

This is the time to make spectacular large-scale arrangements in church because many tall plants are available, including Acanthus mollis and A. spinosus. These perennials, long-lasting both as a plant and a cut flower, have dramatic spikes although the flowers themselves are quite inconspicuous. They make a good background for more colourful flowers but the leaves should be removed because they wilt at once. The flower heads are heavy and are best arranged in a deep container with a double support of a pinholder and wire netting. They are an exception to the rule of 'cut when young' because they can wilt at this stage and should be cut when the florets are all out. Yarrow (Achillea), up to 4-foot tall, is another must for the gardening flower arranger because the flat yellow heads with a rough texture are excellent when fresh and keep their colour well when dried. Cut these flowers also when mature to avoid wilting.

Other tall stems can be cut from mullein, Verbascum 'Broussa' grows up to 12-feet and the Scotch thistle (Onorpordum acanthium) up to 10-feet. The latter has grey-green stems better picked just before

GOOD RESOURCES *Sheila Macqueen's large arrangement for summer includes flowers of acanthus, large leaves of hostas, onopordum and Phormium tenax with an ornamental cabbage in the centre. Photographer R.M. Pendreigh in Winchester Cathedral.*

flowering and handsome grey leaves, but this plant is prickly and needs careful handling. It is helpful to condition it by first standing it in boiling water. The useful leaves of both plants are better not immersed because the greyness can be lost. Artichoke and cardoon leaves are long and graceful for large arrangements and again should not be soaked. The heads can be cut and dried for winter. The handsome Euphorbia wulfenii, with a height of up to 4 feet, its blue-green leaves and rounded, bright yellow-green flower bracts densely arranged in terminal columnar panicles about 9 inches long, matures from May to July. The heavy heads need the same strong supports as Acanthus but last well. Yucca filamentosa flowers in hot summers with up to 6-foot tall stems; it is spectacular arranged alone. Tall foxgloves are still about and short-lived hollyhocks, delphiniums and the delicate Campanula lactiflora 'Loddon Anna' which grows to 4-5 feet, with mauve-pink flowers which are ideal for wedding arrangements. They last well when the stems are first held in boiling water before being soaked. Enormous gladioli can be invaluable but need a firm stem support because they are heavy. Beech is by now very reliable and long branches can be cut without fear of wilting.

Wild plant material

Ferns are mature enough to use by now and can look elegant and cool. It is best to use older fronds, which will last two weeks. They can look stiff when arranged and those with curved tips are more graceful. An arrangement looks less flat when the ferns are turned slightly, cut to different lengths and placed at a number of angles.

The Common Lime trees are in flower and, stripped of leaves, the branches make lovely outlines for large or small arrangements. The keys of sycamore, Norway maple and hornbeam look attractive when branches are defoliated so that they stand out more clearly. Teasels, common in the south and midlands, can be gathered in the wild, so that they need not be grown in the garden where they can be invasive. Lesser Reedmace or Lesser Bulrush can be cut for smaller winter arrangements. Rosebay willow-herb, called 'Herb of Heaven' in Sweden, is still to be found and there are wild honeysuckles which should be cut when in tight bud. Also useful for trails is Old-man's-beard growing mostly in the south. Corn marigolds are pretty for small short-lived arrangements and so is meadowsweet with charming cream flowers found in wet places. It must be placed in water at once and will last about two days. Fennel, with its acid-yellow dainty flowers, grows abundantly in some places such as Suffolk. It lasts well and can be bunched in masses like Queen Anne's Lace. This plant can also be grown successfully in gardens.

ALTAR FLOWERS

A pair of arrangements on either side of the altar cross can emphasize it in a number of ways, such as by the use of Hogarth curves or crescents turning towards the cross. But crescents turning in the opposite direction can be a change and lead the eye to the centre in a similar way.

LIMITED RESOURCES

City

Niches, alcoves, nooks and crannies are to be found in many old churches. These provide excellent positions for flower arrangements. They draw attention to the flowers because they frame them, but in addition fewer flowers are necessary because the backs and the sides

AVERAGE RESOURCES *Pink carnations, blue scabious, white gypsophila and grey foliage on the communion table, St Martin's, Talk-o-th-Hill.*

LIMITED RESOURCES *Long-lasting city garden foliage providing a background for a few roses and six florists' carnations, photography John Wright, in the Church of St Mary, Warwick*

'The Holly and the Ivy' with red carnations arranged in Wells Cathedral by members of the South West Area of NAFAS. By courtesy of The Flower Arranger

A pedestal arrangement by Jean Taylor in St Wilfrid's Church, Mobberley, using red-flowered horsechestnut with lilies, gladioli, carnations and stock with leaves of artichokes and hostas. Photographer Douglas Rendell. By courtesy of The Flower Arranger

of the arrangements are not important. Very often these niches are at eye-level or higher, and so display the flowers to everyone's view.

In hot sultry weather flowering plants can be a better buy for a city church than cut flowers, but they must be well-watered and dead flowers must be removed. There is plenty to choose from, including tall fuchsias, geraniums and pelargoniums, nasturtiums, lobelias, begonias, marigolds, petunias and long-lasting hydrageas. They can be interspersed with foliage plants such as ivies, ferns, and Coleus, grown for its vivid leaves. Bay trees can be used at the entrance. They are expensive but can be used indefinitely and add something permanently green to the church all the year round. These can be underplanted in summer with flowering plants.

Pot-et-fleurs are as good a standby in hot weather as in cold and a few cut flowers can be added to bowls of plants at the weekends for church services.

Flower arrangers on the church rota may be willing to grow troughs and bowls of flowering plants for use in church during the hot summer months and to be responsible for renewing them as they fade.

LIMITED RESOURCES *Garden daisies with ferns and honesty leaves in an alabaster bowl arranged by Dorothy Berisford. Photography D. Rendell.*

Country

Daisies always look cool and pretty in summer especially in country churches. The size of the flowers of Chrysanthemum maximum (Shasta daisy) or of Chrysanthemum uliginosum (Moon Daisy) is regular. More interest can be provided by adding some smaller flowers from the countryside or garden such as chamomile or feverfew. These repeat the daisy shape but in a different size. Ferns can be found easily and, combined with some plain surfaced leaves, such as honesty or geranium, make a good background for flowers.

Wild flowers, 'the flowers of the field', can certainly be found for country churches throughout July and although the flower arrangements will probably have to be done every two days they cost nothing and are very appropriate.

IDEA OF THE MONTH

The normal triangular arrangements on a pedestal can be somewhat monotonous. For a change the pedestal base can be used in other ways.

When an arrangement can be made at floor level, it can join up with an arrangement on top of the pedestal, so that flowers carried down on

GOOD RESOURCES *Two arrangements with a swirling effect arranged by members of the South West Area of NAFAS. One is in blues and yellows and the other in reds, pinks and white. Photography D. Rendell.*

162

one side join up with flowers carried upwards from the arrangement at floor level. The result is a gentle swirling effect which can look very beautiful. Both arrangements should be made in concealed containers painted with dark paint so that they do not stand out. A candle can be incorporated in the top arrangement.

This style could also be used at Christmas with evergreens and a candle. A few red carnations or white lilies could be added for a contrast. For Easter evergreens could contrast with garden daffodils, single yellow chrysanthemums or lilies.

The shape can be made full or slender according to the amount of plant material used in the design. Where it is not practicable to use a container at the base, a parcel of soaked Oasis in thin polythene could be tied to the base of the pedestal (in two places for stability) to hold flower stems.

SPECIAL OCCASION FLOWERS

There are a number of ways of using flowers for special occasions. Few or many flowers can be used. Accessories, which should be appropriate for church use, can be selected for their suitability for the occasion. A cope is always a favourite accompaniment because present-day embroiderers have done some beautiful work, both modern and traditional, in lovely colours. The flowers should be suited to the pattern of the embroidery so that both are in harmony. Colours, shapes and even flowers can be echoed.

The shape of the arrangement can emphasize the character of any accessory used so that a curving shape, to symbolize motherhood's protection, may be perfect for a statue of the Madonna and Child.

FESTIVALS AND SAINT DAYS

July 2 The visitation of the blessed Virgin Mary
It is on this day that the Western Church commemorates the visit of Mary to her cousin Elizabeth who was pregnant with St John the Baptist. This visit is seen as symbolic of kindness because Mary's journey was difficult. Elizabeth said the words 'Blessed art thou among women, and blessed is the fruit of thy womb'. This day could be remembered with an arrangement of simple flowers around a statue of Mary.

July 25 St James The Greater
This James was the brother of John and a fisherman in Galilee in

GOOD RESOURCES *A cope with a complementary arrangement in blue and white by members of the South West Area of NAFAS in Wells Cathedral. The leaves were painted blue in this modern arrangement. Photographer D. Rendell.*

GOOD RESOURCES *The memorial statue to Mrs Helen Dere, Diocesan secretary to the Mothers Union, by Josephine de Vasconcellos, surrounded with flowers arranged by Mrs Coulthurst, Mrs Jackson, Mrs Singleton and Mrs Bailey of the Longridge Flower Club. Photographed in Blackburn Cathedral by Westminster Studios.*

partnership with Andrew and Peter. At the call of Jesus he 'forsook all and followed Him'. When the Apostles went out two by two, James and John went together. He became the patron saint of Spain because legend says that he preached in Spain before he was martyred in Jerusalem in AD 43. His shrine, after Rome and Jerusalem, became the most popular place of pilgrimage and his badge, a scallop shell, was the badge of medieval pilgrims. Scallop shells could be incorporated into an arrangement interpreting this Saint's day.

FORWARD PLANNING

The summer soon slips away and flower arrangers are left only too quickly with gardens lacking much choice of plant material for church arrangements. July is the most important month for preserving and drying plant material for winter.

Preserving

This term refers to the absorption of glycerine to replace water in plants. It keeps them supple and in shape, although there is a colour change from green to a shade of brown ranging from cream to almost black. Leaves of deciduous trees are mature in July; maturity is essential because young cuttings do not absorb glycerine. There are a few flowers and seedheads which can also be treated. A chemist can order a large jar of glycerine at lower cost than many small bottles.

Mix a quantity of glycerine with twice as much hot water and stir well. Scrape and split the stem ends of woody branches and slit hard stems for about 2 inches (5 cms) before placing them in the hot glycerine and water solution. About 3 inches of stems should be in the solution. Topping up may be necessary if the container runs dry before the leaves have turned colour.

Exact times for leaving the leaves in the solution are impossible to state because much depends on the variety of leaf, the temperature of the room and the maturity of the branch. Thinner leaves are ready more quickly than thick ones. The colour of the leaves changes gradually from fresh green to brown or a bronze-green and this is a good indication of when preservation is complete. No harm is done by

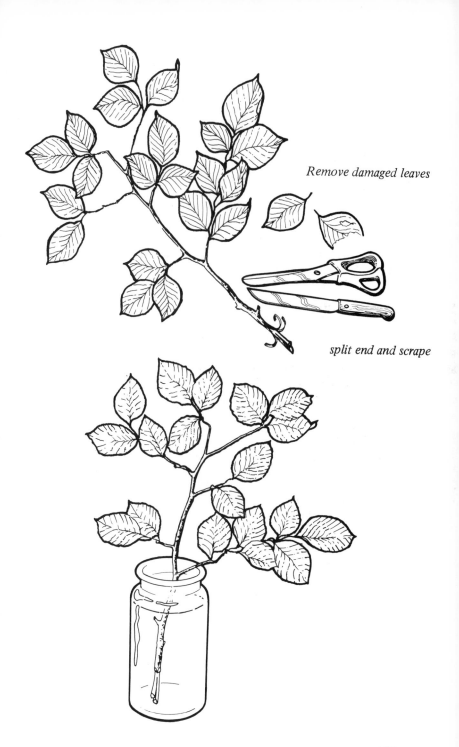

Remove damaged leaves

split end and scrape

Foliage can be glycerined in July for use in winter. This arrangement includes aspidistra, mahonia, beech, grevillea and grasses in shades of cream to brown.

leaving them too long in the solution. If some oozes through the leaves a quick swish in warm soapy water will remove excess glycerine and avoid stickiness.

Stand in glycerine solution during this month:
Branches of beech both green and copper, escallonia, oak, sweet chestnut, apple, forsythia, whitebeam, cotoneaster, lime tree flowers after removing the leaves
Stems of Solomon's Seal after flowering

Old-man's-beard just before the flowers open and after removing the leaves

Mature ferns, which absorb the solution more easily if they are submerged in the solution in a shallow dish

Eryngium alpinum, the flowers of which can be treated when mature but not the leaves

The seedpods of wild irises

Leaves of hostas which can be successfully treated if they are submerged in the solution

Leaves of evergreens may also be treated, but since evergreens are available all year and look so lovely in church in their green state there does not seem much point in turning them brown with glycerine treatment. It is better to save expensive glycerine for useful deciduous leaves.

A range of brown colourings in beech can be obtained by standing the treated leaves in strong sunshine for about two to three weeks.

Drying

Some plants have strong rigid stems and these are the ones to hang up in dry air for a few days to get rid of their water content. Unless

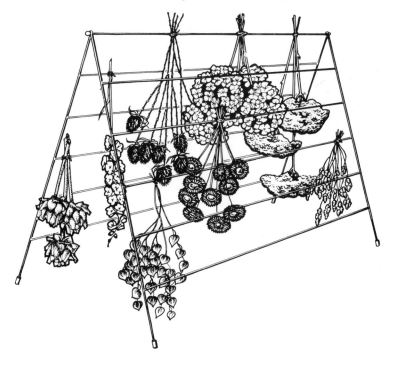

especially strong in the stem, it is better to hang them upside down so that the vertical shapes are retained. Store carefully in a dry, dark place to retain the colours.

At this time of the year dry delphiniums, achillea when mature, acanthus when all the flowers are out or at the seed stage, love-lies-bleeding, sea holly, seedheads of poppies, wild dock, grasses, globe artichoke and cardoon heads.

Experiment with preserving and drying because different flower arrangers are successful with different leaves and flowers. No glycerine is wasted if it is not taken up by a cutting.

Planting
Plant autumn-flowering bulbs during July including Amaryllis bella-donna under the protection of a south or west wall. The pale pink, trumpet-shaped flowers are longlasting and an excellent size and shape for church flower arrangements. Nerine bowdenii, with smaller flowers and strap-shaped pink petals, is also useful and can be planted at the end of the month.

AUGUST

Church flower arrangers in seaside and country churches where there are tourists are likely to be busy in August. Many people enjoy walking round a local church during their travels and fresh flowers give a welcome and the impression that care and interest are taken in the church. In the cities it is a quieter month with many people away on holiday.

Watering the garden continues to be necessary in some parts of the country and temperatures can be over 80°. Sultry weather often ends with a thunderstorm so staking of tall plants is essential. In the north and west rainfall can be heavy during the month and in Scotland and Northern Ireland it can be an autumn month with increased wind and even gales. Special occasions, when extra efforts are made with flowers, are few at this time. But if a harvest or flower festival is to be celebrated in September or October plans should be well under way by now.

Many flower arrangers say that there is 'nothing to pick in the garden' in August, but this is a statement relative to the flowery months of May, June and July; foliage is still excellent for cutting and there are plenty of long-lasting flowers.

PLANT MATERIAL

Florists' flowers
It is a quiet month in most florists shops although there is plenty of choice from gladioli, dahlias, chrysanthemums, scabious, marigolds, carnations, roses, alstroemerias, pyrethrums, asters, lilies, stocks, agapanthus, antirrhinums, sunflowers and a few late delphiniums. Available flowering pot plants are cannas, fuchsias, gloxinias, begonias, hydrangeas and chrysanthemums.

Garden plant material

Lilies
Lilies are a garden feature during this month and my favourite flower for church arrangements. They are spectacular, long-lasting and have a purity of form that is fitting for a church. The lily, considered to be the flower of the Virgin, was generally accepted by Renaissance painters as

171

GOOD RESOURCES *Florists or garden flowers with long-lasting garden foliage including white dahlias, gladioli, carnations, Lilium longiflorum and leaves of aspidistras, bergenias, cupressus and grey Senecio laxifolius arranged at the foot of the royal pew in the Queen's Chapel of the Savoy by Joan Golland, Photographer Dennis Barnard.*

the supreme symbol of spiritual radiance and purity. This symbolism lingers on to this day. There are also many references to the lily in the Bible, such as 'consider the lilies how they grow' and '. . . its brim was made like the brim of a cup, like the flower of a lily' (although some think that this lily was a tulip or an asphodel).

The Immaculate Conception by Carlo Crivelli (d. 1495-1500) showing lilies, roses and fruit, reproduced by courtesy of the Trustees of the National Gallery, London.

Lilium candidum, the Madonna Lily or the Cottage Garden Lily as it may be called, flowers normally in July but in late gardens it may be growing still in August. This is the lily of Renaissance paintings, a paragon of beauty and purity.

Lilium auratum, the Golden-rayed Lily of Japan, with huge bowl-shaped flowers and white petals with yellow bands and wine-coloured spots, is perhaps the handsomest of all but 'Black Dragon', one of the Olympic Hybrids, with white inside petals and rich purple-brown markings outside, can carry as many as twelve flowers on one stem.

Lilium longiflorum, so much used for weddings and a flower that can be obtained almost all the year round from florists, has longer trumpets and a classical form appropriate for any occasion. Lilium regale is one of the easiest to grow and has white flowers with yellow centres and rose-purple backs. It continues to bloom year after year. Lilium aurelianense (Aurelian Lily) with large bowl-shaped flowers and others with strap-like petals are bi-coloured, white cream, gold-yellow or pink. 'Enchantment', a Mid-Century hybrid in orange, is excellent for flowering year after year. Lilium giganteum (syn. Cardiocrinum giganteum) has stems 6-10 feet tall and once seen can never be forgotten. What a spectacular sight it would make in a cathedral, but sadly it is rare because a bulb takes four years to flower and flowers only once.

Some lilies cannot tolerate lime so if you have a lime soil you may need to grow them in pots rather than the garden, setting the bulbs as soon as available in autumn in John Innes No.1. A nurseryman might grow lilies specially for the church if garden culture is not practical.

Arranging lilies

No special conditioning is necessary but take care when handling the flowers because the petals can bruise or 'crack' easily. By picking in bud a long vase life is ensured. The yellow anthers can stain clothing as well as the centre of the flower and some people prefer to cut these off immediately, although the flower does lose some of its beauty when the bright yellow is missing from the centre. Light yellow anthers indicate a young flower and dark yellow is a sign of age.

Lilies demand special care when they are arranged because they have such 'star' quality. They can be combined with other plant material, arranged alone on their tall main stem, or cut off the main stem and arranged using the short flower stem only in low bowls.

1 Mixed with other flowers lilies make excellent central emphasis. It is advisable to place them in position early when arranging and to work

other plant material around them so that the large heads are exactly where you want them with plenty of surrounding space to show their forms. Any mechanics can be used.

2 The lilies that grow with many flowers at the top of long stems do not mix with other flowers easily and usually look more beautiful when arranged alone at full height. But they can look top heavy and the addition of a few large leaves of hostas or bergenias near the rim of the container restores visual balance. The lily's own leaves are insignificant when compared in scale to the flowers, but they soften the appearance of the straight stems.

As an alternative to arranging one tall stem with large leaves at the base, try a cascading column made by using three or more stems

one stem carrying many flowers can be arranged alone

—Leaves used at the base of the stem improve the visual balance

175

in one container. Place the stems one behind the other in the mechanics so that from the front only one stem is visible. If necessary tie the stems together in two or three places, using soft green yarn, to hold them in position. See illustration on page 178.

The stems can be impaled easily on a heavy pinholder in a low container, but for extra stability because of the weight of flowers at the top, it is advisable to cover the pinholder with stones or large pebbles, which also conceal the mechanics.

When a tall container is used wire netting can be combined with a pinholder in the bottom. Alternatively a fresh block of soaked Oasis can be pushed into the vase, but try not to put stems in more than once because the Oasis will lose support and an exact vertical position is important when striving for a dignified, uplifting appearance in the arrangement.

3 Sometimes odd flowers are cut off a tall stem with many flowers. A good way to use these up is to mass them in a bowl at the foot of a

a tall stem may need a second support of wire netting

*short stemmed
lilies massed
in a low bowl*

cross or statue. The shape of each individual flower is lost but when the heads are turned in different directions the effect is striking.

In addition to lilies, gardens can produce for cutting agapanthus, achilleas, amaranthus, campanulas, alstroemerias, antirrhinums, asters Acanthus mollis, sunflowers, marigolds, dahlias, stocks, montbretias, Tobacco Plant, phlox, roses, rudbeckias, scabious, Shasta Daisies, eryngiums, zinnias, gladioli, chrysanthemums, larkspurs. Sedum flowers, still in the green stage, are especially useful and last for weeks. They provide a rough-looking texture. Cream-white Artemesia lactiflora (White Mugwort) has useful tall stems to provide a good background for other flowers.

Wild plant material

Teasels, grasses and reedmace (or bulrush) can still be picked and the yellow iris fruits can be cut for preserving with glycerine. Wild angelica, Angelica sylvestris, looking like Cow Parsley, is common and Sedum telephium with the common names of Orpine or Livelong is longlasting because of its fleshy leaves. For tiny arrangements Campanula rotundifolia, the delightful blue harebell or Scottish Bluebell, can be found in dry, grassy places, hedgerows and roadsides, often on poor soils.

Many people enjoy gathering heather, or ling, (Calluna vulgaris) from heaths, moors, bogs and open woods on acid soils. It dries for winter use in small arrangements. In its time it has been used for bedding, fuel, thatching and basketry. The Bell Heather, Erica cinerea and the larger flowered Bog Heather, Erica tetralix, are often found together. The white campion on road verges is a pretty flower thought to have been introduced to this country 2,000 years before Christ.

There are tiny green 'cones' on the alder trees and round fruits on the London Plane (Platanus x hybridus). Black elderberries can be gathered from August to November and it is better to defoliate the branches for longer life. Red berried Guelder Rose (Viburnum opulus) and Mountain Ash or rowan (Sorbus aucaparia) with orange-red berries make colourful additions to arrangements from now until late autumn, but also last longer when defoliated. Bramble sprays are interesting in autumn designs and provide useful sprays.

ALTAR FLOWERS

The simplicity of a single variety of flower can be most beautiful on an altar or communion table. A few white medium decorative dahlias, chrysanthemum blooms, gladioli or lilies, arranged with other foliage if needed, are often more appropriate than a mixture of flowers of many colours. They give a peaceful beauty, simple and uncluttered, a reminder of the beauty of nature but not a dominant feature of the altar furnishings.

GOOD RESOURCES *The altar in the chapel of the Royal Holloway College, Surrey, with stems of yellow lilies. Arranged by Joan Owen against a green velvet background. Photographer Dennis Barnard.*

LIMITED RESOURCES

City

Pine, cedar and larch can be gathered on trips to the country. They are longlasting and an occasional spray of water maintains their freshness. Two stems of Lilium auratum, or several flowers of Lilium longiflorum, or large dahlias or chrysanthemums can be arranged with these branches and a few leaves of bergenias or hostas.

It is a mistaken belief that it is necessary to use many flowers in a church arrangement. This is not so and a simple design can show off the

178

LIMITED RESOURCES – CITY *Two stems of Lilium auratum, two branches of pine and a few leaves of bergenias in simple containers covered in grass matting arranged in the Collegiate Church of St Mary, Warwick, by Alice Kneebone. Photographer John Wright.*

beauty of flower shapes and colours, the textures of leaves and the lines of branches, which can be appreciated far more than when they are combined with many flowers and leaves. Space is an important factor in this style of design so that individual flowers, leaves and branches can be seen clearly.

Existing containers may not be sufficiently large for tall branches and the larger flowers of later summer and autumn. It is an easy matter to buy a drainpipe of a suitable size from a builders' merchant. It is possible to find one with an attractive mellow colouring. Alternatively a covering can be made, and glued to the surface, of bamboo matting or split bamboo canes. Another type of texture can be applied by using stone-coloured paint containing sand. A drainpipe is not water-proof because it is open at each end, but it is a simple job to drop a plastic or tin container into the top to hold water and mechanics.

Country

August is a month when informal arrangements are appropriate in a country church. A branch of larch can be used for height with ferns, rhododendrons or other leaves as a background for flowers and to cover a bowl of water and mechanics. There are many varieties of flower which could be used for emphasis in the centre but those with a rounded shape provide more impact. A base of a natural material such as wood, stone or slate is in harmony with this style of arrangement, which brings the beauty of the countryside into the church in a charming manner.

IDEA OF THE MONTH

Floral tapestries or carpets have become a feature of flower or harvest festivals in recent years. They attract many visitors to the church and are a style of decoration that can be arranged by volunteers who are not expert flower arrangers. With the wealth of plant material available during September and October they need not be expensive. August, if not before, is the time to plan such a project.

Good organization and timing are essential to the success and some-one should be on the committee who is experienced in pattern planning, such as a fabric designer.

There are two basic ways of assembling the tapestry:

1 It can be accomplished in one session with many people working together at one time on a plan designed beforehand

2 Separate units can be arranged, with flower and leaves, in the homes of many volunteers and brought to the church at a given time for assembling into an overall design according to a prepared plan.

LIMITED RESOURCES – COUNTRY *Larch, ferns and rhododendron leaves with Golden Marguerite flowers (Anthemis tinctoria) arranged in a concealed container on a crosscut of polished wood by Jean Taylor. Photographer Douglas Rendell.*

Method 1

It is necessary to have containers for the mechanics to avoid spillage or siphoning on carpets or wooden floors. Plastic seed boxes or trays without holes in the bottom are suitable. Fill these with moss, Oasis or wet sand and wrap each one in thin polythene to avoid leakage and hold in the moisture. Assemble them together on the floor. Mark out the pattern first, using sprigs of yew, pegs or string pegged in place, and following a plan previously designed. Add flowers over the yew, using a sharp implement or a skewer to make holes through the polythene for stems that are not woody or strong. After the pattern outline is completed, and this is better worked out by only a few people, fill in the contrasting background of plain colours. Flowers or foliage can be used around the edge to hide the seed boxes.

GOOD RESOURCES *A carpet of flowers 32' x 5' in celebration of the Queen's Silver Jubilee, using 5,000 white carnations and a pattern of yellow roses by a group of flower arrangers from the South Midlands Area of NAFAS.*

Method 2

Plan the pattern on graph paper, basing it on a square module or unit size, which could be an 8-foot (20 cms) square foil freezer case. When all the separate units, filled with flowers, are placed together the tapestry is formed. The mechanics in the foil case can be a large block of Oasis cut in two lengthways, or soaked moss if economy is necessary.

A floral tapestry 40' x 20' arranged for the Golden Jubilee of the Diocese of Leicester, contributed by Dorothy Cooke. By courtesy of the Leicester Mercury.

Each volunteer must be given a paper on which the pattern is drawn for a particular units or units. Each unit should be numbered according to the overall plan so that quick assembly is ensured later. The colours should be marked and possibly the type of plant material.

At an appointed time the units are delivered to the church and assembled by a small committee working from an overall numbered plan. The tapestry grows rapidly as the units are placed together. The floor can be protected with a sheet of polythene or tarpaulin. It may be necessary for the committee to insert foliage around the edge of the tapestry to conceal the sides of the foil cases.

A section of the overall plan with the dotted square depicting one unit.

SPECIAL OCCASION FLOWERS

On some occasions each flower arrangement in a festival can be different in style, colour, shape and size. On other occasions and in some places reptition of an arrangement can give a sense of unity and provide continuity. Certain positions lend themselves to this, such as pew ends, a series of ledges, window sills, pillars and the front of choir stalls.

AVERAGE RESOURCES *Repetition of arrangements of garden foliage and roses in a small chapel in the Collegiate Church of St Mary, Warwick. Arranged by Mary Watson and Heather Tomson. Photographer John Wright.*

LIMITED RESOURCES *A spray, of garden foliage and berries with florists flowers, on a pew end in the Collegiate Church of St Mary, Warwick. Arranged by Kathleen Hedgecoe. Photographer John Wright.*

An expert flower arranger can make up a model for those who are not so experienced to copy, using similar plant material; this should be allocated beforehand so that everyone has the same quantity of each variety of flower and leaf. When a party of people work together at one time, the arrangements are easier to match.

As a change from using the same shape, style, size and colour, the arrangements can vary in size while remaining the same in other ways. Or they could look similar in colouring and a colour scheme could use cream at one end of a nave, yellow in the centre, deepening to gold at the other end.

FESTIVAL AND SAINT DAYS

The quiet month of August could be a good time to start planning next year's flower festival. Many thousands of pounds have been raised through festivals during the past twenty-five years which have enabled urgent restoration, maintenance and the purchase of new furnishings to be undertaken. There can be few churches, chapels or cathedrals that have not held at least one flower festival. There is no decline in their popularity for both flower arrangers and the visiting public who continue to flock to all festivals with joy and interest.

Ideas and details of how to organize a festival are in chapters 10, 11 and 12 of *Flowers in Church*, but committees enjoy staging something new each time. In early festivals colour was a major interest and the harmonizing of flowers with stained glass windows, church furnishings and the vestments of the clergy. Historical people and events connected with Church, the town or city have been represented with interpretative arrangements, the Saints have been depicted often, and hymns and carols illustrated. The Church Year can provide a theme and special services such as those for Baptism and Mothering Sunday. But for those searching for new ideas the Bible is an unending source.

Some people in the church will know suitable texts from the Bible, but to save research a Bible concordance is invaluable. A concordance is an index of words or passages. It is probable that there will be one in the church and if not they can be found in libraries. There are many to be bought at various prices, according to size, from religious and other book shops.

References are easy to follow with usually an alphabetical arrangement of words for quick reference, and the book chapter and verse where a text or word can be found. For example, references can be found to texts that include lilies and other flowers, vines, colours, the sea, gardens, birds and animals.

The words or passages interpreted with flowers can be kept to an overall theme. There should be cards professionally printed giving each text so that visitors can learn and admire the interpretation. This can be an excellent way of making the Bible more familiar to people, and adds meaning to flower arrangements instead of displaying only their decorative value.

Topical Bible Concordance, Lutterworth
Cruden's Complete Concordance, Lutterworth
The R.S.V. Handy Concordance, Pickering & Inglis
The Bible Readers' Encyclopaedia and Concordance, Collins
Oxford Encyclopaedia Concordance
A Handy Concordance to the Bible, Pickering & Inglis
Concise Bible Concordance, Hodder & Stoughton
Concise Dictionary of Religious Quotations, Mowbray
The Oxford Dictionary of Saints, OUP
The International Standard Bible Encyclopaedia, Eerdmans
The Lion Encyclopaedia of the Bible, Lion Publishing
Festivals and Saint Days, Blandford
A Year of Festivals, Frederick Warne
Customs and Traditions of England, David and Charles o.p.
The Christian Calendar, Weidenfeld & Nicholson
Folklore and Customs of Rural England, David and Charles

FORWARD PLANNING

Gardens
Order new perennials, bulbs for pots and lilies this month. Plant Lilium candidum and daffodils by the end of the month. Chrysanthemums should be disbudded for larger blooms for church arrangements. Ornamental cabbage seeds can be sown.

Preserving and drying
Montbretia leaves can be preserved to provide a dark brown sword-like leaf in winter. They can also be pressed under a carpet with success. Ferns and bracken can also be pressed but they tend to be brittle. Many of the flowers and leaves mentioned in the chapter for July can still be preserved or dried during August.

SEPTEMBER

September is the first of the autumn months when fruit begins to ripen and the dahlias and chrysanthemums are in full bloom. The warm, dry weather still continues but temperatures are rarely high. The nights are cooler and more humid, causing dew and mists to form readily with occasional light frosts in the early morning.

Harvest festivals may be held towards the end of the month and it is a favourite month for flower festivals as many people are still either on holiday, or enjoying one-day outings. Looking at festival flowers gives great pleasure and attendances are high. Flowers are plentiful in the shops and much cheaper than at any other time in the year, another important reason why flower festivals are popular in September.

PLANT MATERIAL

Florists' flowers

Late summer flowers are found according to local sources and weather conditions, but dahlias, chrysanthemums in variety, carnations, roses, Michaelmas Daisies, gladioli in many colours, stocks and lilies with freesias, anenomes and lily-of-the-valley for small arrangements, are normally in the shops. Flowering pot plants of chrysanthemums, cyclamens, heathers, the Christmas Flower (Poinsettia pulcherrima) and fruited capsicums can be bought.

Garden plant material

Although gardens are beginning to look rather weary, there is still much that can be cut. Anenome japonica has a delicate flower which lasts well in smaller arrangements and combines easily with blue scabious. Tobacco plant and phlox, Michaelmas daisies, stocks, asters, sea hollies, roses, nerines, love-lies-bleeding and campanulas provide material for arrangements that look more like summer with their blues, mauves, pinks and white. But there are many flowers in autumn colours of orange, red and yellow, including zinnias, marigolds, roses, the Mexican Sunflower (Tithonia), an annual with brilliant orange flowers, alstroemerias, heleniums, red hot pokers, gaillardias, gladioli, chrysanthemums, rudbeckias and achilleas.

AVERAGE RESOURCES *Chrysanthemum blooms, carnations and gladioli with aspidistra leaves for a long-lasting arrangement which can be made in country or city churches. Arranger Joy Fleming. Photography Pictone Studios.*

Spectacular designs are possible using larger dahlias, gladioli, acanthus, hydrangeas and sunflowers. Sedum is green, or turning pink, and lasts for many days providing an interesting rough texture. Another tall green stem is Molucella laevis (Bells-of-Ireland) which can be three feet tall if grown in a greenhouse, though smaller if out-of-doors.

Nothing looks more beautiful than a massed bowl of autumn-flowering gentians in a blue which is distinctive anywhere, contrary to the usual receding blues. Fruits are now available, and one of the most

190

dramatic is Phytolacca americana (Poke Weed or Red-ink Plant). The dark purple, almost black, fruits look like blackberries on an upright stem but are poisonous if eaten. There are also fruits of berberis, coton-easters, crab apples, pernettyas, Mountain Ash and viburnums. Foliage is also plentiful and reliable in September. There are as yet no autumn colourings but there is a large variety of long-lasting green leaves.

Arranging dahlias

Brilliantly coloured dahlias are everywhere, but they have bare stems and unsuitable leaves for arrangements and are usually better when combined with other leaves to soften the appearance of the stems. Iris leaves provide pleasant contrast with dahlias which otherwise have a dominating round form. Whenever possible cut or buy when some of the flowers are half open so that there are graded sizes. The tight buds of dahlias are not as attractive as the half-open flowers.

Some of the stems are hollow and when you cut these it is a good idea to fill them with water and plug them with a tissue. Dahlias need care when travelling because the heads can be knocked off easily. They can be laid so that the flowers are on crumpled tissue paper, or stood in a bucket of water. When carried in a tight bunch the flowers tend to get damaged.

A bowl of only one variety, especially of the water-lily shape, looks very beautiful when arranged in graded sizes with other foliage such as hosta and iris.

Arranging hydrangeas

Hydrangeas are likely to wilt quickly if immature but as they grow older they last well. Cut a flower with a woody stem. Standing the stem end in one inch of boiling water is helpful before a deep soak for two hours or more. Placing the head in a polythene bag is beneficial when soaking because this retains moisture in the flower. If the blooms are young it is important to spray them occasionally with water or to lay wet tissue paper on them overnight. Older flowers will last for weeks in water, eventually drying out for winter decorations.

WILD PLANT MATERIAL

There are berries and fruits to collect. Lords-and-Ladies has red fruits for small arrangements. Mountain Ash or rowan has clustered red berries; it grows on moorlands and at the foot of mountains. There are black fruits on the Wayfaring Tree (Viburnum lantana) which grows on dry, chalky soil, and red berries on the Wild Guelder Rose which appears in ditches and damp hedgerows. Hawthorn berries are plentiful but rather a dull shade of red. Fairly common in the south is Stinking Iris or Gladdon, a native perennial of hedgebanks, damp woods and sea cliffs, with brilliant orange-red fruits that form in the autumn and last until spring.

Heather and Urpine, or Livelong, can still be found and there are harebells and the Bluebells of Scotland — flowers ascribed, like many others, to the devil, goblins and witches.

There are cones, hazel nuts and Horse Chestnut 'conkers' and winged seeds on the Silver Birch, and small hanging fruits on lime trees. The seedheads of several of the Umbelliferae family can be cut and protected from bad weather indoors. When undamaged they can be glittered and are useful for Christmas arrangements, as well as for autumn designs.

A pair of arrangements for the altar of a small church. They can be placed facing in either direction to emphasize the cross.

ALTAR FLOWERS

The shape of arrangements on the altar can be varied, depending on the effect you wish to achieve. A pair of symmetrical arrangements, whether triangles, circles or ovals, has a formal, motionless appearance, sometimes seemingly unconnected with the cross in the centre. Asymmetrical

Garden flowers and foliage arranged in May in an alabaster container by Veronica Gibbs. Photographer Allan Hurst

LIMITED RESOURCES – COUNTRY *Foliage with a few stems of flowers arranged in Winchester Cathedral by Mrs W. Lutyens. Photograph by R. M. Pendreigh. By courtesy of The Flower Arranger.*

LIMITED RESOURCES – CITY *Dahlias arranged in the Queen's Chapel of the Savoy by Florrie Wolfe. Photograph by Dennis Barnard.*

194

shapes can draw attention to the cross but have more visual movement and therefore seem less formal. The tallest stems in asymmetrical curves can be on the outside or on the inside of the arrangements; either way they can emphasize the cross.

LIMITED RESOURCES

Country
Few flowers are necessary when plenty of foliage is used. At this time of year it is especially long-lasting and will outlive flowers which can be renewed from time to time. Garden chrysanthemums will last many days but dahlias will need replacing more often. A teaspoonful of mild disinfectant in the vase water will prevent it from smelling unpleasant.

City
Larger arrangements can be made at little expense in September. Dahlias, in all their glowing shades of orange, red, pink and yellow, are easy to come by. There should be foliage available in flower shops but, if not, glycerined foliage (especially light brown beech leaves) looks lovely with the autumn shades of dahlias.

IDEA OF THE MONTH

A festival of flowers in a cathedral or very large church will often have space for a symbolic emblem specially drawn for the occasion and using something associated with the cathedral in the design. The emblem, with flowers, can be repeated throughout to link the decorations and provide a sense of continuity. It would be too much to include an emblem in every flower arrangement but it could be placed in several positions and also be printed on the festival brochure and on publicity matter. It is advisable to ask an expert to design it.

SPECIAL OCCASIONS

For a huge spectacle at a flower festival, in a cathedral, or in a church with lofty roofs, arrangements can be made about twenty feet high. The foundations must be very firm and the whole construction completely stable. The help of handymen is advisable. The taller the arrangement, the bigger and heavier must be the base. If it does not entail hammering nails or screws into the fabric of the church, a really safe decoration is achieved by wiring it to a pillar, wall or other permanent feature.

AVERAGE RESOURCES *The emblem used for Winchester Cathedral Flower Festival designed by Pamela McNicol. Photograph by R. M. Pendreigh. Flowers arranged by Mrs M. Faulkner.*

GOOD RESOURCES *A twenty-foot arrangement for the Queen's Silver Jubilee, in the Collegiate Church of St Mary, Warwick, arranged by the members of Knowle Flower Arrangement Club. The mechanics were a tripod and cross bars of aluminium tubing with planks placed across in three positions to hold one, two and three bowls as the arrangement broadened. Work started from the top with the arrangers standing on scaffolding. By courtesy of The Flower Arranger.*

FESTIVALS AND SAINT DAYS

It is an especially successful month in which to hold a flower festival. The organization of flower festivals and the making of large size arrangements and special effects are covered in *Flowers in Church*, pages 98 to 144. Some churches hold the harvest services in September.

Pulpits and fonts

AVERAGE RESOURCES *The pulpit in Siddington Church arranged for harvest festival by Mrs Kennerley and Mrs Reeves. Photographer D. Rendell.*

The pulpit and the font are favourite positions for flowers when festivals are held. They are rarely alike and individual treatment is necessary in every church. It is important to avoid obscuring hand-carved wood or stone work which should be complemented by the flowers.

If you have no special mechanics it is worth discussing with the flower guild how these should be made. A local joiner or metal worker

AVERAGE RESOURCES *The pulpit arranged by members of the Barrow-in-Furness Flower Club in St Paul's Church, Barrow, with blue and peach flowers. By courtesy of* The Flower Arranger.

GOOD RESOURCES *The font with white gladioli and single chrysanthe-mums arranged by members of Lymm Flower Club in All Saints Parish Church, Daresbury. The unusual font needed special care.*

can make containers and devices for holding them in position. No damage should be done to the wood or stone work and permission should be obtained for any construction. Some flower arrangers protect the pulpit with felt and polythene but this may be unnecessary if flower holders are positioned where there is no likelihood of damage. An especially ornate pulpit may only need flowers on the ledge which holds the reading stand but these should flow outwards and not restrict movement in the pulpit itself.

September 21, St Matthew

Matthew was also known as 'Levi' and was a wealthy tax-collector and customs official at Capernaum. Consequently he is the patron saint of bankers and tax collectors. But he may be difficult to interpret with flowers. His festival is one of the most ancient and was mentioned at Rome in the fifth century. Matthew became the evangelist in Palestine and then probably in Ethiopia, Parthia and Persia. He became honoured as a martyr.

September 29, St Michael the Archangel

The feast of St Michael was renamed 'St Michael and All Angels' at the revision of the English Prayer Book in 1662. Michaelmas is the ancient English name for the feast when it was a popular festival and holy day of obligation. Many customs were linked with this day in particular the eating of the Michaelmas goose. Michael is the patron saint of artists and soldiers and an interpretative arrangement could combine flowers with a painting or a soldier's hat.

FORWARD PLANNING

Planting

Shrubs can be planted at the end of the month. If not already available, valuable shrubs for the church flower arranger are Spotted Laurel, Elaeagnus, Golden Privet, Rhus cotinus, hollies, thujas, Whitebeam, mahonias, camellias, bay trees, ivies, Rosemary, cotoneasters and skimmia and Griselinia littoralis for light green leaves, Choisya ternata and rhododendron for dark green clustered leaves; escallonias, forsythias, hydrangeas, buddleias, weigelas, viburnums, brooms, lilacs for flowers; snowberries, pernettyas, pyracanthas and cotoneasters for berries; ornamental plums, peaches, cherries and almonds for blossom. Eremurus and alliums should also be planted now.

Bulbs

Pots and bowls of bulbs can be planted for Christmas flowering. It is important to buy those specially prepared for Christmas. Hyacinths and tulips should be planted in early September and daffodils and narcissi by the end of the month.

Preserving and drying

Achillea adds invaluable colour to winter arrangements and should now be mature enough to cut and dry by hanging in a dry room. Love-lies-bleeding, Bells-of-Ireland (Molucella laevis) and sea hollies can be preserved with glycerine. Hydrangeas can be cut and dried by standing them in an inch of water as soon as they begin to feel papery, they can also be glycerined to turn them a silky brown. Helichrysums (Straw Flowers) should be cut and wired if this has not already been done. Gourds can be harvested and dried in the airing cupboard; they can be used in arrangements and then returned to the cupboard. Eventually they become completely dry and honey coloured. Unless they are dried they will probably become mouldy and then have to be discarded but dried gourds last indefinitely. It is not too late to preserve other deciduous foliage with glycerine.

OCTOBER

October may have lovely weather, especially in the middle of the month when there is often a mellow Indian summer. The fruitfulness of autumn and the changing colours of foliage add to this hazy beauty. Many harvest festivals are held to make this a busy month for flower arrangers. However there is inexpensive plant material in quantity unless there are early frosts.

This is an important planting season for bulbs and hardy herbaceous plants for cutting for church arrangements next year.

PLANT MATERIAL

Florists' flowers

There is an assortment of late summer and autumn flowers available; including dahlias, chrysanthemums, gladioli, nerines, Michaelmas Daisies and a few delphiniums, gerberas and alstroemerias. There are Lilies-of-the-Valley and Kaffir lilies for small arrangements; exotic anthuriums and freesias; irises and anemones, normally associated with spring; not forgetting the all-the-year-round carnations, lilies, spray chrysanthemums and roses.

Plants of azaleas, capsicums, chrysanthemums, cyclamens, heathers, the Christmas flower (Poinsettia pulcherrima), primulas and Winter Cherry are also available.

Garden plant material

Bulbous Amaryllis belladonna (Belladonna Lily), one of the most beautiful flowers, grows at this time and although it belongs to the daffodil family, its appearance is more like that of a lily. The large trumpet-shaped, rose-pink or white flowers grow on bare stems and need the protection of a south, or west facing wall in the midlands and north. Nerine bowdenii, the hardy nerine, blossoms reliably and needs protection only in the coldest areas. Heads of rose-pink flowers with irridescent, strap-shaped petals appear on foot high stems. They are dainty rather than solid in appearance and make a change from the usual autumn colourings and heavier shapes.

GOOD RESOURCES *Florists' carnations and chrysanthemums with fruit and wheat placed high on a pillar for easy viewing, arranged by Jean Hill in Leicester Cathedral. Photograph by Neville Chadwick.*

GOOD RESOURCES *A large arrangement can be made less expensively in October. Arranger Mrs Randall in Southwell Minster. By courtesy of The Flower Arranger.*

Alstroemerias, Red-hot Pokers, Michaelmas Daisies, border chrysanthemums, dahlias, gaillardias, heleniums, rudbeckias, Chinese Lanterns and antirrhinums in all their rich glory can still be cut, while phlox, scabious and Tobacco Plant have a few remaining flowers.

Foliage is turning colour everywhere, but sadly some leaves, especially maples, do not last when cut. A life of one or two days in an arrangement is as much as can be expected from leaves with changed colour, although those with a larger proportion of green can last longer. Especially beautiful are leaves of Mountain Ash, Virginia Creeper, Fothergilla major, Smoke Tree (Rhus cotinus), Tulip Tree (Liriodendron tulipifera) and Parrotia persica. Green beech leaves turn bronze and can last well.

As the autumn advances there are many colourful fruits in the garden. The cotoneasters have red, orange, yellow or purplish-black berries; some of the more common survive through winter without being eaten by birds. Other fruits include white snowberries; white, pink, purple and red pernettyas with short stems; Mountain Ash, with bunches of orange berries, which are quickly eaten by the birds (although they do not take white, pink or yellow ones so readily); ornamental crab apples; pyracanthas with orange and red berries in clusters; Celastrus orbiculatus, a climber with brilliant scarlet seeds in yellow capsules which are long-lasting; berberises; Skimmia japonica with persistent brilliant red berries when there are male and female plants (although it is an erratic producer); and roses with hips, such as Rosa rugosa and Rosa moyesii.

An inedible ornamental grape vine, Vitis coignetiae, has black fruit with a purple bloom and leaves with rich autumn colouring. They look magnificent with red dahlias or roses. Hypericum has black fruits for small arrangements.

Treatment of berries

It is not possible to preserve berries although their life may be extended by spraying with a clear varnish. For a special occasion branches can be cut earlier and placed in water in a cool place until wanted. A large polythene bag placed over the berries will hold in moisture and fatten the berries.

For the same reason, and to prevent birds from eating them, a polythene bag can be tied over berries growing on a tree.

Stems of cotoneaster and pyracantha berries can be stood in a solution of one part glycerine and two parts hot water for two or three days to lengthen their lives.

Wild plant material

Although the countryside is turning brown and dry stems stand starkly against the bare sky, there is still bounty to be collected. Elderberry foliage in the most subtle and beautiful colourings can be found and its black fruits are rich-looking. Other useful fruits are wild crab apples, dog rose hips, blackberries and snowberries. There are hazel nuts, often called filberts after Saint Philibert of Jumieges in Normandy who died in AD 684. Wild hops are dry on hedges and along thickets and there are prickly-cased horse chestnut fruits, the conkers beloved by children. The Sweet Chestnut has spiny burrs containing red-brown nuts and clusters of these can be used in arrangements and preserved with glycerine. Sprays of ash keys can be collected; it was believed that the ash protected people from evil and that ash keys should be carried to guard against witchcraft.

Bryony, with red berries and yellowing leaves, and Old-man's-beard, can be cut in trails if carefully disentangled from the undergrowth. Velvety reedmace (bulrush) can be collected if you have long rubber waders because it normally grows at the edges of lakes, ponds, canals and slow-moving rivers. A spray of clear varnish is necessary at this stage of growth to prevent the seeds from unrolling and blowing. Bulrushes are invaluable for height in winter arrangements. There are plenty of cones to be gleaned from the foot of firs, pines, cedars, spruces and larches (see also page 248).

CHURCH WINDOW FLOWERS

Church windows often seem a natural place for flowers but it is difficult to see them against the light, and their beauty is only apparent when night falls. Sometimes an arrangement can be placed at the side of the window still where most of it may be seen against a wall. For a flower or harvest festival a background can be made and placed behind the flowers. This should not obscure beautiful stained glass windows but is acceptable in front of a plain window. A neat, unobtrusive backing can be made with hardboard or strong cardboard, covered in either neutral-coloured hessian for a country church or velvet for a city church. Hardboard can also be painted, using a soft colour; several coats being necessary for a good finish.

When window sills are non-existent or sloping, an arrangement of flowers can be made in a polythene parcel and hung from the window bars (see *Flowers in Church* page 132).

GOOD RESOURCES *Flowers complement a stained glass window in Heslington Church, arranged by Pauline Mann. Photograph by D. Bonsall. By courtesy of The Flower Arranger.*

AVERAGE RESOURCES *A background placed between the flowers and the light in Heslington Church. Photography by D. Bonsall.*

LIMITED RESOURCES *A country arrangement of flame dahlias, orange chrysanthemums and countryside beech, crab apples, burnt teasels and pheasant feathers with peppers and grapes on a wooden base. Grasses could replace the dried palm in the centre. Arranged by Hugh Mather. Photographer H. Leadbetter.*

City

Bunches of border chrysanthemums can be bought at low cost from florists, markets and barrows during October. Massed together in an all-round arrangement they can look very effective when placed high up and hung from a bracket. An Oasis parcel can be used but avoid making holes in the underside to prevent leakage. An alternative method of supporting the flowers is to use a hanging basket with a concealed container in the centre.

Country

Only a few flowers are necessary when fruit, seedheads, driftwood, grasses and foliage are used in autumn. Arrange all other material first, then place the flowers carefully because they will be a dominant feature. At this time of year there are many gleanings to be made in country lanes.

IDEA OF THE MONTH

As an extra decoration for flower and harvest festivals, or in churches with high walls and suitable positions, a row of banners can be hung. Dried flowers and preserved leaves can be arranged on a length of felt with a band of braid, or fringe to tidy the end. A curtain rod, slotted through a hem in the top and embellishments of painted wood or plastic add a heraldic touch. A rope with tassels increases the overall effect.

SPECIAL OCCASIONS

A festival of any kind provides an opportunity to display vestments belonging to the church or borrowed from other local churches. Beautiful embroidery is seen on many copes, both modern and traditional. It is important that the flowers and the vestments harmonize in colour, style and shape of the design. To raise the grouping and keep the vestment off the floor, they can be staged on a covered plinth.

Other beautiful objects such as paintings, pottery, local crafts, wood carvings, antiques and sculptures can be combined with flowers and featured from time to time on special occasions and at regular church services. This engenders anticipation and interest in the church members and brings the artistic world into the church life. Exhibits should be chosen with discrimination so that they blend with the interior of the church.

LIMITED RESOURCES *Border chrysanthemums massed in a hanging basket for a city or country church. Arranger Mollie Bailey in Siddington Church. Photographer D. Rendell.*

AVERAGE RESOURCES *Dried and preserved plant material glued on to a banner of gold felt, designed by Nettie Roth.Photograph by Dennis Barnard in the Royal Holloway College Chapel.*

GOOD RESOURCES *A traditional arrangement in autumn colours complementing a rust coloured cope in the Collegiate Church of St Mary's, Warwick, by Stratford on Avon Evening Flower Club. Photographer John Wright.*

FESTIVALS AND SAINT DAYS

Harvest festival

Most churches are decorated in thanksgiving for the harvest. Gifts of flowers, harvest produce, tinned and packaged food are blessed in the church and then taken to hospitals, children's homes, old people and those in need. The church service is a joyful occasion and one of the best attended of the year, often with special music and hymns, and extra decorations in addition to the gifts.

Present day church harvest festivals have developed through the church's interest in harvest customs, many ancient in origin. Before Christ there were rituals concerned with the renewal of life. Early man thought that by cutting his crop he might have killed the Spirit of Fertility and that a ceremony was necessary to ensure the renewal of growth the following season. It was thought that this spirit retreated into the last ears to be cut and the responsibility for cutting these was often shared. In many rituals the last corn was then formed into a model effigy or doll in which the spirit could take refuge. The sheaf might be dressed in women's clothes bedecked with ribbons and called the harvest queen, the kern baby, the neck or the corn doll. At other times it was twisted and woven into a man's shape tied with ribbons at the waist and neck.

Corn dollies made by Raymond Rush for the harvest festival at Siddington Church. Photographer D. Rendell.

The effigy or corn idol was then carried joyfully to the home farmstead where it was given a place of honour throughout the winter and protected from the weather, birds and pests. In the spring another happy procession took the effigy back into the fields and broke it open to release the spirit into the newly sown grain. Until quite recently corn dollies have decorated ricks at harvest time as they were thought to ward off witches and evil spirits. Corn dollies are still popular today and it is an expanding craft. Small ones are made in traditional named shapes and used for general decoration and interest, and not for their former role. They can be used in churches for the harvest festival and many parishes have experts who bring them each year to the church.

Harvest-home is a celebration of bringing in the harvest with farmers and their helpers enjoying good food, singing and merriment as the last corn is cut. The church's interest in harvest customs led to greeting the harvest with a peal of bells and later to the blessing of produce in the church. A corn dolly graced the church door but eventually this became a cross of corn stalks.

The Reformation discouraged this but in 1843 the Vicar of Morwenstow invited parishioners to receive the Sacrement in the bread of the new corn and the modern tradition of harvest thanksgiving was begun.

Harvest Festival decorations

There is an abundance of flowers and fruit at this time, making its organization and arrangement quite difficult, especially because gifts continue to arrive all day long during the preparation of the church. However, a place is always found for everything.

Gifts

It is probably a good idea to concentrate all gifts, which will later be given to people in need, in several places. Large baskets and wheelbarrows can be filled, or tables covered in hessian to hold tinned and packaged goods. Heavy vegetables and fruit such as large marrows, melons, cauliflowers and cabbages can be grouped together on the floor in corners of the church. Eggs look decorative when heaped in strong deep baskets and so do rosy-red apples. Grouping things of a kind together gives a greater sense of order. In turn, the smaller groupings can be placed together in several bigger groups of gifts.

Decorations

The organization of the gifts can be a separate task from the organization and arranging of the church flowers. Some planning and preparation ahead of time is helpful. If possible find out what flowers may be given on the day so that they can be incorporated with those planned beforehand.

One way of achieving order from what can so easily be chaos is to sort all the gift flowers into shapes such as tall and spikey flowers and leaves, other foliage, round flowers, trailing stems and 'filler' flowers. Alternatively colours can be grouped together and arrangements made in shades of one colour. When colours are mixed, bronze, orange, flame, red and yellow are the ones usually available. They are also suitable for the time of year. A touch of brilliant deep pink, found in dahlias and gladioli, can add life to rusts and reds. Plenty of yellow is advisable in a dark church because it shows up well.

Arrangements of one kind of flower only can be spectacular. Michaelmas Daisies, gladioli and chrysanthemums are suitable but dahlias are not and look better mixed with other flowers or leaves.

Trailing sprays of blackberries, crab apples and other fruits and berries can be included with flowers. Larger fruits can be impaled on dowel sticks. Ornamental gourds are especially striking although they cannot be eaten later. Large hanging decorations of fruit, berries, a few

AVERAGE RESOURCES *Flowers at eye level attract attention. Red and green arrangements at a festival in St Martins, Talke.*

AVERAGE RESOURCES *Hugh Mather's arrangement of gladioli, dahlias, fruit and foliage could be made for a city or country church using laurel in place of houseplant leaves. Photographer H. Leadbetter.*

flowers and leaves look effective. They can be arranged in a parcel of Oasis. Wire netting over the parcel is advisable so that heavier fruits can be wired to it and also a loop of wire can be attached for hanging over a pew end or choir stall.

Arranging fruit

Flower arrangers who have not included fruits in their designs before may wonder how to go about it. Some people use wire but this spoils the fruit for eating later, unless it is twisted on to the stem only. Dowel stick if washed well can be used with one end pushed into the fruit and the other into Oasis or wire netting. It does little damage to the fruit. A slight downwards angle when inserting the fruit into the arrangement prevents it from dropping off the stick.

You can make a grouping of fruit beginning with a grapefruit in the centre. Build it up by impaling the other fruits into the grapefruit and into each other; use more than one stick if necessary. By placing fruits of the same variety together in small groups a more orderly effect is achieved. Elongated vegetables and fruit, such as carrots, bananas, courgettes and also grapes can be used at the extremities of an arrangement with the more solid shapes in the centre. There is also less confusion when stems point in the same direction. Contrasts of texture, shape and colour provide more interest.

A few leaves in small tubes of water placed amid the fruits can soften the appearance of an arrangement. Glycerined foliage can be tucked in the gaps without tubes.

Cereals

Cereals are often used symbolically in harvest festival decorations. Small bunches can be inserted into flower arrangements. Several stems wired together make more of a feature than single stems scattered amongst the flowers.

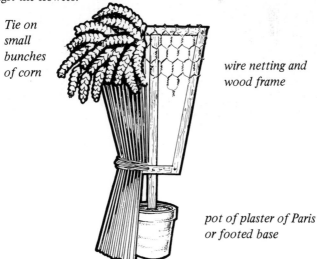

Tie on small bunches of corn

wire netting and wood frame

pot of plaster of Paris or footed base

AVERAGE RESOURCES *Metal cones with flat backs and holes for wire at the top hold flowers for a garland effect in Siddington Church. Simple corn dollies are tied with ribbons on the pew ends. Arrangers Mrs Mollie Bailey and Mrs Roy Wain, corn dollies Raymond Rush. Photographer D. Rendell.*

A sheaf of corn must be ordered from a farmer ahead of time; it has to be made specially because a combine harvester does not make sheaves in the same manner as former machinery. In place of a sheaf, corn can be tied to a wire netting foundation held upright by a frame of wood with a footed base for support. Begin to tie small bunches at the top and overlap them gradually until the top part of the netting is covered. The stems only should show at the base and the 'waist' can be tied with plaited raffia or ribbons. Fruit and vegetables can be banked around the base to conceal it.

A local baker may be willing to bake an attractive loaf which can be placed on the altar table or in a window. An interpretative grouping can be made and include a sack of corn seed, sheaves, flour, bakers' tools and farmers' implements with one or more loaves of bread.

Hassocks of flowers

Often there are too many flowers for arrangements and hassocks could be made with shorter stemmed varieties. Cut a large block of Oasis lengthwise into three and place them on top of a length of cling-film wrapped over an upturned seed box. Add extra Oasis if necessary to cover the box. Do not cut off the roll of wrapping because another length should be drawn across the top of the Oasis to make a parcel. Cut off the surplus at this stage, and neaten the parcel by folding the wrapping over.

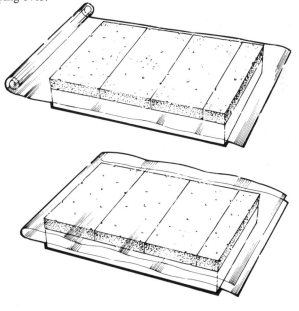

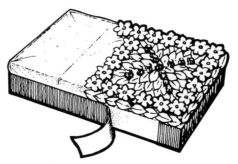

Add flower heads on short stems, making holes with a skewer or knitting needle. A pattern can be formed with flowers using flat leaves to fill the spaces between. They can be held in place with long pins concealed by overlapping leaves. Finally pin a wide ribbon, preferably velvet, around the edges to conceal the box.

The kneelers can be positioned to form a carpet or used separately on steps or in front of the choir stalls.

Other harvests

It is interesting to interpret other harvests such as the harvest of the sea with blue hydrangeas, green and grey foliage, driftwood and fishing nets with floats. Grapes, vine leaves, baskets and wine can be arranged for the grape harvest, apples and flowers for the cider crop, dried flowers and preserved leaves for the flower arrangers' gleanings and so on.

Saint Theresa of Lisieux, October 3

Saint Theresa was often called The Little Flower because of her saying 'I have never given the good Lord ought but love and it is with love that He will repay. After my death I will let fall a shower of roses'. She died aged twenty-four in 1897 after a life of simple faith. Her day could be remembered with a bowl of roses.

Saint Francis of Asissi, October 4

Francis who preached to the birds and loved the flowers also kissed and cared for lepers. His followers became the largest religious order in the world, the Franciscans. Although he was born into a wealthy family he lived with the poor as one of them. The children in the church would be interested in a landscape scene including small model animals and, if available, a statue of Saint Francis.

Saint Luke, October 17

Saint Luke's day would be an opportunity for displaying a painting with flowers because he is the patron saint of artists and also of doctors.

Either of these could be represented in an interpretative arrangement.

FORWARD PLANNING

Bulbs and corms

This is the time for planting bulbs and corms which have not been planted in September. Useful for the church flower arranger are alliums, alstroemerias, the Belladonna Lily, the Crown Imperial, montbretias, hyacinths, nerines, tulips and arums in milder parts of the country. Clivias, hippeastrums and vallota (Scarborough Lily) can be planted in pots and an exciting plant, eucomis (Pineapple Flower), has green flowers and could be useful for special occasions. Arums in white, and yellow can also be potted-up in colder areas.

Hardy herbaceous plants

The soil is still warm and not too wet in October and is ideal for planting hardy herbaceous plants except in the coldest and wettest parts of the country. Descriptions are given under March, the other planting time. Plants useful for cutting for the church include Acanthus mollis, achilleas, anthemis, Michaelmas Daisies, astilbes, astrantias, Macleaya cordata, campanulas, Chinese Lantern, Christmas Roses, Pampas Grass, globe artichokes, Crocosmia masonorum, delphiniums, pinks, perennial foxgloves, doronicums, erigerons, sea hollies, euphorbias, gaillardias, grasses, heleniums, sunflowers, hostas, red hot pokers, Pachysandra terminalis (for foliage), peonies, poppies, phlox, pyrethrums, ranunculus, rudbeckias, scabious, sedums, senecios, globe flowers, Verbascum bombyciferum, Vinca major (periwinkle). Your local garden centre is sure to have some of the plants listed.

NOVEMBER

This is not an easy month, coming as it does between the last of autumn's bounty in October and the anticipation of Christmas in December. Armistice Day brings sadness and memories. The days are often cold, foggy and raw with some occasional snow in the north; although in the southern part of the country wintry weather comes later.

If there are no frosts, some flowers can still be cut in the garden, but if they arrive there is a dearth of garden flowers overnight and flower arrangers must think differently about plant material for their designs.

Preparations for Christmas can begin when the weather keeps people indoors. It is not too early to plan the church decorations for the festival period; later everyone becomes busy with the many activities of Christmas.

PLANT MATERIAL

Florists' flowers
There is not a lot of choice because the season is between the autumn flowers and the bulk of the spring flowers. There are still alstroemerias, nerines, anemones, freesias and lily-of-the-valley for small arrangements, chrysanthemums in variety, lilies, carnations, gerberas, gladioli, roses and a few dahlias. Arching stems of Euphorbia fulgens arrive; they have small scarlet bracts in terminal sprays. Blue iris from the Channel Islands and Holland are available but the gentle blue does not show up well in church.

Pot plants of chrysanthemums, azaleas, gloxinias, heathers, cyclamens, poinsettias (Christmas Flowers), polyanthus and Solanum (Winter Cherry) and the usual foliage plants are available.

Garden plant material
The flower arranger cannot depend on garden flowers any longer, although nerines, sedums, chrysanthemums, roses, hydrangeas and even geraniums and dahlias may be found until the frosts arrive. There are colourful leaves at the beginning of the month but they last about

AVERAGE RESOURCES *Grasses, dried, blue hydrangea, evergreens and fresh peach-coloured chrysanthemums arranged by Enid Degenhardt in the chapel of Royal Holloway College. Photograph by Dennis Barnard.*

a day indoors. Evergreens and berries with a few florists' flowers become the standby. Colourful fruits of holly, arbutus, berberis, callicarpa, cotoneaster, pernettya, euonymus, crab apple, yellow and red pyracantha, skimmia, sorbus, snowberry, Chinese Lantern and viburnum can still be cut to add sparkle to an arrangement of a few flowers. Catkins should be available from Garrya elliptica and Lauristinus (Viburnum tinus), an evergreen, has small white flowers touched with pink which can start to bloom in November. Ivy has creamy-green flowers despite the weather. The Kaffir Lily, a bulbous plant, has small pink or scarlet star-shaped flowers growing in sheltered places. There are yellow Winter Jasmine flowers and polyanthus, seemingly out of season, for small arrangements.

Wild plant material
Only evergreens in the countryside now show that life in the plant world is still continuing. Most of the trees are again showing their skeletons of branches; elderberries hang heavily and soon drop from their stems; red hips and haws stand starkly against the sky but are often weather-damaged by now. Old-man's-beard or Traveller's Joy silvers the wayside in the midlands and south and long trails can still be cut but are not long-lasting.

The impression of growth coming to an end is everywhere but is belied by the tiny buds appearing on bare branches which show that the marvel of the life-cycle continues.

LIMITED RESOURCES

City
Glycerined foliage in many shades of brown seems appropriate for a late-autumn, early-winter month, and now repays the small amount of work involved in preserving leaves during the summer.

Make a background of foliage before adding flowers and less will be needed. The rough visual texture of chrysanthemums and carnations mixes well with smooth, light brown beech leaves and a large arrangement can be made for little cost. Dried grasses, seedheads and flowers can be included.

Country
Garden flowers dried during summer can be made into gifts to sell at a church bazaar. Small trinket boxes and frames especially made for dried plant material can be bought, or an inexpensive mount can be made.

LIMITED RESOURCES *A large arrangement can be made with three chrysanthemum blooms, six carnations and preserved beech leaves. Arranger Jean Taylor. Photographer D. Rendell.*

Cut strong cardboard to shape or use a small cakeboard. Cover with fabric, such as hessian or velvet, by glueing with UHU at the back. Nick the edge of the fabric where necessary, so that it lies flat and pull the cover tightly intp place. Neaten the back with Fablon after taping on a loop of cord, or ribbon, for hanging. A small calendar can be added. Complete the arrangement to your satisfaction before glueing it into place.

LIMITED RESOURCES *The dried flowers of summer made into a plaque by Renee Mottershead and photographed by H. Leadbetter. By courtesy of The Flower Arranger.*

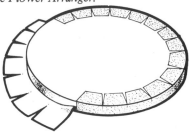

GOOD RESOURCES *Houseplant foliage arranged by Hugh Mather. Photographer H. Leadbetter. Garden foliage in similar shapes could be substituted.*

ALTAR FOLIAGE

It is normal to think in terms of flowers for altar arrangements. But foliage can be equally beautiful and often longer lasting. The patterns, shapes and textures of leaves can be as fascinating as flowers. The formality of leaves from houseplants suit an elegant, large church, but garden foliage can be just as decorative in a small, more informal church.

Whatever the source of leaves the same guidelines apply to arranging them. Tall, slender forms give height and dignity. A rosette shape or a lighter, brighter or patterned surface gives emphasis at the centre. A variety of differing shapes, textures and colourings adds interest but this does not mean that many of them should be used in one arrangement; repetition of a few of these gives an arrangement more unity.

Try adding half a soluble aspirin to a pint of water to extend the life of a foliage arrangement. The solution helps to close the pores which are normally open in green leaves during daylight. This cuts down loss of water through the pores and the leaves last longer, especially in a dry atmosphere.

IDEA OF THE MONTH – decorated passages from the Bible

Flower festivals are not normally held in November, but in this quiet month some decorations can be made and stored for a festival the following year, when dried and pressed flowers and leaves will be used. Visitors to festivals spend time examining arrangements in greater detail than normal, and it is most interesting to include some small designs in addition to larger decorations.

One suggestion is to use a lettering pen or a lettering system (e.g. Letraset) to write a passage from the Bible on heavy paper the same size as the church Bible. Tiny pressed or dried flowers and leaves can be glued to the pages, like the books of hours which were so lovingly and delicately illustrated with painted flowers by monks in the middle ages. The delicate beauty of pressed flowers attracts wonder and admiration. The sheets of paper can be positioned without damage to the pages of the opened Bible.

SPECIAL OCCASIONS

Armistice Day
This is a very special occasion in November and churches all over the United Kingdom remember those who gave their lives for others in two world wars.

AVERAGE RESOURCES *A passage from the Bible decorated with pressed and dried flowers by Mrs Gwen Corrin in the Collegiate Church of St Mary, Warwick. Photographer John Wright.*

It is appropriate to emphasize war memorials at this time with fresh or dried flowers, or with red silk poppies and foliage. It is important to avoid obscuring the names on the memorial and flowers should be added as a complement. In a country church an interpretative design can be made with a cross of simple branches.

232

AVERAGE RESOURCES *An expressive cross of branches with barbed wire arranged above red silk poppies and laurel leaves by Joan Lancaster and Sally Mungall in St Mary's Church, Thornthwaite, Cumbria. Photographer G. Partington.*

GOOD RESOURCES *Red roses and green foliage arranged around the memorial in St Paul's Church, Barrow, by members of the Barrow-in-Furness Flower Club.*

LIMITED RESOURCES *A cross for Armistice Day using cones of many sizes glued to a polystyrene base strengthened with bamboo canes, arranged by Ella Park in St Mary's Church, Thornthwaite. Photographer G. Partington.*

A large arrangement but few flowers

Large arrangements do not need a large number of flowers because a few can be combined with preserved or fresh foliage and dried seedheads and grasses. Green and brown leaves are an interesting combination and, if you wish, a few flowers can be added to provide more contrast. Larger flowers are more in scale with artichoke heads, big leaves and tall, fluffy grasses. There are dramatic red, pink or white anthuriums which are expensive but can last a month; their shiny texture is an effective contrast with the rough texture of grasses. Exotic strelitzias in orange and blue, and large chrysanthemum blooms are also a suitable size.

FESTIVAL AND SAINT DAYS

November 1, All Saints Day

November 2, All Souls Day

Hallowe'en on October 30 has retained many of the pagan 'black magic' elements of early festivals and has little or no authority in the Church, but All Saints and All Souls Days have great meaning for Christians.

All Saints Day is a celebration in honour of Saints, known and unknown; a recognition of the many devout Christians whose good works are worthy of sanctification but who are unnamed or unnumbered in the Christian calendar. It is a day when Christians attend the service of Eucharist or Communion.

On All Souls Day the Church remembers all those who have died and such commemorations are mentioned as early as the third century. Simple white lilies are appropriate for this day. Arrangements for All Saints Day could interpret the lives of the Saints or their workers because many are Patron Saints.

November 22, St Cecilia

This Patron Saint has an untraced connection with music, although it is thought that she sang as she died, martyred for her Christian faith, in AD 176. There is also a legend that her singing attracted an angel to earth. Musicians adopted her as their Saint in the middle ages and subsequent festivals of music held on her day have inspired great works by composers. Flowers could be combined with a musical instrument on this day or for a music festival.

November 30, St Andrew's Day

Andrew, a fisherman and the brother of Simon called Peter, was one of

GOOD RESOURCES *A spectacular design of red anthuriums with dried and preserved leaves, grasses and seedheads arranged by Mary Tyler. Photographer R.M. Pendreigh.*

GOOD RESOURCES *A dramatic design of large leaves and Pampas Grass, with little need for flowers, by Majorie Wilson and Audrey Rimmer at Holker Hall. The euphorbia heads belong to early summer but chrysanthemum blooms or large dahlias with stems in tubes could be used. Photographer Peter Joslin. By courtesy of The Flower Arranger.*

GOOD RESOURCES *Flowers can be arranged around a musical instrument for a service of special music or on St Cecilia's Day. Arrangement by Mrs Crosher and Mrs Parsons in Southwell Minster. Photographer by Lead, Nutt and Stevens. By courtesy of The Flower Arranger.*

the twelve apostles who followed Jesus. He was crucified for being a Christian but he elected to die on a cross of the form 'crux decussata', or diagonal, maintaining that he was not worthy to die as Jesus had died. This has become known as St Andrew's cross.

He is now the Patron Saint of Scotland, and legend says that his relics are buried there, although another legend says that they rest in Italy. In the Scottish flag, his cross is white for purity with a blue background for the sea he loved. Scottish people all over the world celebrate St Andrew's Day.

An interpretative arrangement depicting Andrew the fisherman could be appropriate using blue hydrangeas and white chrysanthemums, or white flowers on a sea-blue base.

FORWARD PLANNING

It is not too early to start planning Christmas decorations for the festival season. If there is to be a flower festival during the following year, plans can begin also for this.

Planting for church arrangements should be continued, including lilies, tulips, hyacinths, trees, shrubs and perennials.

DECEMBER

The month of December has a sense of anticipation and excitement. There are many church activities including carol singing and social events as well as special church services. Decorations for the Christmas festival should be planned early in the month, if not before, because the church flower arrangers have a busy time in many ways at this time of the year.

The weather is variable with fog and frost inevitable at times and colder weather setting in at the end of the month; however this does not affect church flower arrangements of garden material because there are few flowers to cut. But inevitably it makes florists' flowers more expensive because of the great demand at a time when extra heating is necessary for producing blooms.

Evergreens, fruit, cones, Christmas trees, candles and lamps take pride of place during this month and there are many delightful ways of decorating the church in keeping with Christmas and without the necessity for garden flowers or many florists' flowers. My own preference is for evergreens in all their many shades of green. They are traditional and with lamps or candles can provide a lovely setting for Christmas services.

PLANT MATERIAL

Florists' flowers

There are carnations, roses, lilies, gladioli, gerberas and Kaffir Lilies, chincherinchees and nerines for small arrangements. The first spring flowers are in the shops and there are anemones, irises, daffodils, narcissi and a few tulips. Sprays of yellow, fluffy mimosa, packed and sold in polythene bags, are not practical despite their beauty, because of their short life. There are many varieties of chrysanthemum including sprays and large blooms.

Holly and skimmia with red berries are sold and there are many varieties of foliage including graceful, long branches of Western Hemlock (dark green on one side and silver on the other), longlasting shiny camellia, laurel, cupressus, box, rhododendron, pittosporum, pine, fir and mahonia.

GOOD RESOURCES *Lilium longiflorum can be bought all year and is often traditionally used at Christmas. Arranger Dorothy Marriott. Photographer Dennis Barnard.*

There may be expensive but long-lasting exotic strelitzias and anthuriums, but traditional flowers are the choice of most people with

GOOD RESOURCES *In a city church houseplant foliage with long-lasting red anthuriums provide Christmas colours for many days. Arranger Hugh Mather. Photographer H. Leadbetter.*

red or white carnations the most popular flowers for combining with evergreens.

There are many pots of bulbs and flowering plants such as hyacinths, daffodils, narcissi, cinerarias, chrysanthemums, cyclamens, azaleas, the Winter Cherry (Solanum capsicastrum) and, favourite of all, the Christmas Flowers or poinsettia (Euphorbia pulcherrima). Many pots of bulbs and flowers are given as gifts, but they can also be used in groups in a church.

The Christmas Flower

Of the varieties raised in recent years, one has short stems but large bracts and another has small bracts. The flowers are small and insignificant, but the conspicuous bracts with a petal-like appearance can be red, white or pink. Red is the favourite for Christmas but the other colours are gaining popularity.

A humid, cool atmosphere is preferable for these plants and in a warm, dry living room they soon drop their leaves; spraying with water is helpful. The bracts and leaves should last until well after Christmas in the cooler atmosphere of a church. In February the stems can be cut down and will grow new leaves in time, but few people are successful in obtaining coloured bracts the following season and the plants are usually discarded.

Stems can be cut from the plant so that the coloured bracts can be used in arrangement without the roots. But the stem ends must be burnt in a match, gas or candle flame, otherwise the white milky sap leaks out and clogs up the stem end making water uptake difficult. The sap is an irritant to sensitive skins and dangerous if it gets in your eyes.

The bracts do not wilt easily when left on the plant, but this cannot be guaranteed when the stem is cut, so perhaps it is safer to use the plant rather than cut stems for church decorations, unless you can check them regularly.

When resources are good, several plants can be banked at different heights against a pillar, pulpit, lectern or choir stall, or in corners of the church. Evergreen in bowls, or in parcels of Oasis, can be placed around and between the poinsettias to make a larger grouping.

A poinsettia plant can make a dramatic centre for a large pedestal of evergreens. The plant can be removed from its pot into a polythene bag. Position this in a large container on a pedestal and then place Oasis or wire netting around the plant to hold long branches of evergreens.

Carnations

Carnations are more suitable for smaller arrangements because so many are required in a large pedestal design that it becomes an expensive decoration. Red carnations can look dull in the dimmer light of a church, especially if the lighting is fluorescent. To give life to an evergreen and red carnation arrangement, try adding yellow-green or variegated foliage, such as ivy, holly, elaeagnus, spotted laurel or euonymus. White carnations show up better than red, so much so that they must be carefully positioned in clusters or in a gentle curve in the centre, otherwise they appear as uncoordinated 'blobs' of white from a distance.

Chrysanthemums

Large white or yellow blooms are effective in big arrangements, but again they should be placed with care. A walk to the back of the church will enable you to assess the effect. Large bronze blooms, unless of a pale shade, do not show up well, but the lovely cream-pink 'Shantung'

LIMITED RESOURCES *Two stems of spray chrysanthemums with holly and candles in candlecups on a candelabrum, a long-lasting economical arrangement, and candles and flowers are easily renewed. Arranger Jean Taylor. Photographer D. Rendell.*

is often available at this time and looks beautiful with glycerined leaves in several shades of brown and with silver backed leaves of Elaeagnus pungens. There is a large single bloom available at this time in white with a yellow-green centre called 'Shastra' which is especially striking with holly and ivy.

White or yellow single chrysanthemum, and the thread-petalled 'Rayonnante', sprays can be used either in a line, in a curve or in an S-shape in the centre of evergreens.

Garden plant material
Evergreens in all shades (see January) and with varying textures are indispensable. Golden conifers, including thujas and cupressus, shiny-leaved camellias and magnolias, yellow-splashed elaeagnus and euonymus, blue-green junipers and Cedrus atlantica 'Glauca' are very beautiful for Christmas. Long before Jesus was born, evergreens played a special part in pagan winter festivals and in homes and shrines, because they were green and living whilst all else was dead. Romans decorated their homes with evergreens in honour of Saturn, god of all things that grew. Christians carried on decorating with evergreens and gave Christian meaning to them.

Holly and ivy
Holly and ivy, the traditional decorations, are used everywhere. It has been thought that holly came from the word 'holy', but it derives its name from the ancient 'holm' or 'hulver' often retained in place names. Nevertheless, holly is associated with 'holy' because its prickly leaves are like the Crown of Thorns which German legend says was of holly, the scarlet berries are remindful of drops of Christ's blood and it was in early days 'proof against the evil eye'. It is associated more recently with foresight.

Ivy is also a plant of antiquity and was prized by the Greeks and Romans. It was associated with Bacchus or Dionysus as it gave potency to new wine, but was also an antidote for drunkenness, and in the Middle Ages a 'tod' or bush of ivy was the sign of an alehouse or tavern and known as an Alepole. Today it is associated with tenacity and friendship in adversity.

Arranging holly and ivy
Plain, dark green holly looks uninteresting but there are variegated ones including the reliable and outstanding Ilex x Altaclarensis 'Golden King' without prickles. Ilex aquifolium 'Argentea Marginata' with silver margins; I.aquifolium muricata (bicolour) and I.aquifolium 'Handsworth

'New Silver'. Ilex aquifolium 'Madame Briot' is one of the best variegated hollies and has berries, and there is the very yellow and striking
I. aquifolium 'Aureo Medio Picta', or the Golden Milkboy or Golden
Milkmaid Holly. Ilex Altaclarensis 'Lawsoniana' has a boldly variegated
leaf.

There are also variegated ivies and trails of these soften the appearance of a pedestal. Hedera canariensis 'Variegata' has silver-grey borders
and H. Colchica 'Variegata' is marked with cream-yellow and pale green.
Larger leaves can be used to hide mechanics.

Look for curved branches of holly and ivy because they are more
graceful and easier to arrange than those with stiff, erect stems. They
are more likely to be found at the back of a holly tree or underneath
where growth is spindly. Occasionally small sprays of plain yellow grow
and these are useful for emphasizing the centre of an arrangement.

Red-berried hollies are normally used, but for a change there is the
yellow-berried Ilex aquifolium 'Bacciflava' which is striking when
combined with yellow or white chrysanthemums. Holly varies in the
amount of berries it carries from year to year according to weather
conditions.

Birds can eat holly berries before Christmas unless you cut them two
or three weeks earlier. Branches can be kept in a bucket half-full of
water covered with a polythene bag and with the ends tucked into the
bucket. This stops birds and mice from eating them and holds in the
moisture. Store the bucket out-of-doors or in a cool outhouse. The
berries become plump and the leaves stay fresh.

The leaves often grow in clusters around the berries, hiding them
from view, so cut off some of the foliage to reveal them.

Christmas Roses

Helleborus niger was known in medieval times as the Flower of St
Agnes, but Christian legend tells how, when the Magi came with gold,
frankincense and myrrh, a poor shepherd girl wept because she had
nothing to bring to the baby Jesus. A passing angel saw her tears and
as they lay on the ground turned them into Christmas Roses for her to
give.

They are especially beautiful winter flowers and are copied in plastic
and used frequently with evergreens and pine cones. But it is appropriate to have real flowers in a small arrangement at the foot of a statue
of the Virgin Mary or in a small arrangement on the altar. Unfortunately
they are very variable plants and do not always appear in the garden on
time. But they can be encouraged by applying a thick mulch of damp
peat all over the crown of the plant in early November. This gives

warmth and ensures longer stems. The opening blooms should be protected with cloches.

They are also variable with regard to conditioning. Some wilt in hours and others keep several days. Those with thicker stems seem to last better. It is important to ensure that water reaches the top of the stem as soon as they are cut. Place in a container of water as you cut and then hold the stem ends in boiling water for a minute or two in the house, followed by plunging them in tepid water as deep as the stems for a few hours. They seem to last better arranged in deep water instead of Oasis.

Other plant material

Berries of cotoneasters are a substitute for holly and although not traditional they do provide a red berry and are not eaten so quickly by the birds; again some leaves will need to be removed. The big white snowberries of Symphoricarpus albus hang on for many months and are fascinating in winter arrangements because they look like miniature snowballs. Skimmia japonica's scarlet berries are brilliant when you can find a shrub with them. Mahonia's yellow flowers, Winter Jasmine and the first winter heathers are pretty in small arrangements. Bowls of prepared bulbs for Christmas flowering, planted in early September for hyacinths and tulips, and early October for daffodils and narcissus, are a great standby in late December and last well, although you may prefer traditional winter designs instead of anticipating spring so early.

WILD PLANT MATERIAL

Cooler weather, long nights and brief days are not the ideal conditions for wild flowers and growth is over. Evergreens can be found including the common holly, ivy, mistletoe, fir, and pine and box on a few chalk and limestone escarpments.

Wherever there are conifers, cones can be collected for Christmas decorations. They can be wired and sprayed lightly with gold, copper or silver paint or left their natural colour to harmonize well with evergreens. Japanese Larch (Larix kaempferi), a deciduous conifer with small cones like brown roses, looks very pretty when the branches are sprayed with a clear varnish and immediately sprinkled with silver or gold glitter, like frost.

The Corsican Pine (Pinus nigra maritima) has rough cones 3 inches long that are easy to wire and can be clustered in groups, and the Scots Pine (Pinus sylvestris) has 2 inch cones. The Bhutan Pine (Pinus wallichiana, syn. P. griffithii) has long soft cones and three make a good

AVERAGE RESOURCES *Snowberries and carnations with begonia leaves (bergenias could be substituted). Arranger Hugh Mather. Photographer H. Leadbetter.*

AVERAGE RESOURCES *A variety of brown cones and seedpods can
be glued to a triangular wooden shape for an everlasting plaque. A light
dusting of gold may be appropriate for Christmas. Arranger Doris Tonge.
By courtesy of the Lancashire Evening Post.*

cluster. The Maritime Pine (Pinus pinaster) has beautiful cones 6 to 8 inches long.

There are Giant Silver Fir cones and the larger European Fir cones and those of the Norway Spruce (Picea abies) which are papery and not so easy to wire. The cones of the Cedar of Lebanon are more difficult to find but are very beautiful when cut with a branch of the tree.

ALTAR FLOWERS

Many churches traditionally have white flowers on the altar at Christmas, sometimes combined with holly. Another idea would be a small, rooted, cone-shaped conifer in a brass, copper, silver, stone or ceramic decorative outer pot. This could be especially suitable for a city because it looks formal, but adds something green and growing to the church. A suitable conifer can be found from a walk round a garden centre or nursery. Suggestions are a small 'pyramid' box, a yellow-green Chamaecyparis pisifera 'Plumosa Aurea' about 2 feet tall, a darker green Chamaecyparis lawsoniana 'Fraserii' about 2 feet 6 inches, dark blue-green 18-inch Chamaecyparis lawsoniana 'Elwoodii'. A pair of any of these should cost no more than flowers. A blue juniper, Juniperus communis 'Compressa' is a lovely colour and a tight conical bush, but it is likely to be expensive and two 8-inch ones would cost a lot more than flowers. However, a rooted bush can be planted later in the church garden or sold to someone in the congregation. Another alternative is a Christmas fir tree with or without a root, but it would have to be really small because of the spreading branches.

Before Christmas the conifers can be unadorned, but for the festival season they could be decorated with tiny gold baubles if the church is ornate with a lot of gold plate. Alternatively for a more natural look they can be hung with small cones, or a few flowers in orchid tubes could be inserted into the foliage.

LIMITED RESOURCES

City
A cone-shaped design can be made of florists' foliage using a base of wire netting and soaked moss or Oasis. This can be prepared several weeks before Christmas, wrapped in thin polythene and stored in a cool place or out-of-doors.

Method. Cut a triangle of 1-inch mesh wire netting and wire the edges or twist the cut ends together to make a cone. The size should be

LIMITED RESOURCES *A conifer with roots can be decorated for Christmas and planted later. Dull gold baubles are restrained and effective. With good resources available several trees could be used.*

LIMITED RESOURCES *Formal trees with foliage predominating arranged in the entrance to the Quire in Wells Cathedral by members of the South West Area of NAFAS. Photographer D. Rendell.*

determined by available space and resources. Remember that the completed cone will be several inches bigger in diameter than the wire netting when the plant material has been added. Also, it can be placed on top of a container to give it additional height, in this case it should be wired to the container for stability.

Fill the wire netting cone with soaked moss or Oasis and fold over the netting at the bottom to contain it. If necessary wire on a circle of netting. Insert short sprigs of foliage such as golden box, plain green box, pittosporum or yew. Any woody-stemmed, small-leafed foliage is suitable. Holly is not advisable because the leaf is large and prickly and can fall out of the cone easily.

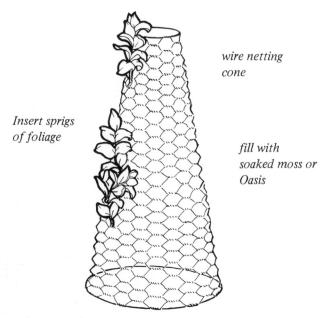

wire netting cone

Insert sprigs of foliage

fill with soaked moss or Oasis

Flowers can be added immediately before the festive season begins. They can be inserted in a random pattern or in circles, spirals or vertical lines. Small wired pine cones and fruit can be an alternative or an addition. Satsumas and small apples can be impaled on skewers inserted at a downward angle to prevent them from rolling off (see also *Flowers in Church*, page 118). Against a background of a wall or church furnishings few flowers are necessary in a cone.

LIMITED RESOURCES

Country

Evergreens, especially holly and ivy, are lovely in a country church with lamps or candles. Driftwood can also be used to stretch an arrangement. A plant of the Christmas Flower or poinsettia with the roots in a polythene bag can be placed close to the wood with a small container of water and mechanics to hold evergreens.

IDEA OF THE MONTH

The use of garlands of leaves and flowers stretches back through history. It was a favourite mode of decoration for the Greeks and Romans. During the middle ages in this country it was used with simple beauty;

LIMITED RESOURCES *Poinsettias with driftwood, ivy and flowers of echeveria (evergreen foliage could be substituted) for a long-lasting informal arrangement by Hugh Mather. Photographer H. Leadbetter.*

just a few flowers bound together for a priest to wear on his head or round his neck on major feast days, a custom which continued until the Reformation. In places such as Hawaii, garlands greet the visitor and in Thailand they are sold, ready-made, by the wayside. It is a natural style of decoration, starting with the simplest of all, the daisy-chain, a childhood delight. Garlands for a church must be more firmly made, but they are especially suitable because they enhance the building without hiding features that are already beautiful in themselves.

For the Christmas festival season they can be made of evergreens in a number of shades and textures; a group of church flower guild members can soon make several lengths and enjoy working together. Evergreen

AVERAGE RESOURCES *A garland of evergreens with a few flowers in St Wilfrid's Church, Mobberley. Photographer D. Rendell.*

GOOD RESOURCES *A garland of foliage and fruit arranged by Mrs M. Maklin and Mrs B. Scott in Beverley Minster for a festival. Photographer J. D. Simson.*

garlands can be made several weeks ahead and stored, wrapped in polythene, out of doors or in a cool place. An occasional spray of water helps them to last well. Flowers and berries can be added just before the garlands are hung in the church, or after positioning, if you can reach them.

A simple foundation is made of 6-inch wide thin polythene of any desired length. Sew it into a tube using a long stitch on a sewing machine or by hand-stitching. Push in small blocks of soaked Oasis or moss and tie like a string of sausages so that the garland will bend.

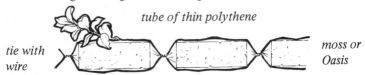

tube of thin polythene

tie with wire

moss or Oasis

Evergreens such as cupressus, box, laurel, yew, with woody stems about 2½ inches long, can be quickly inserted at a slanting angle to cover the polythene. Avoid making holes which will cause drips when the garland is hung. Spray chrysanthemums, cut with a stem about 3 inches long, can be inserted in a few places, using a meat skewer to make holes; this prevents the stem from bending as it is pushed in. Wired cones, berries and small fruits impaled on sticks can be used. Other methods of making garlands are described on pages 120-122 of *Flowers in Church.*

Garlands can be looped horizontally or vertically in many places in church, but they can be quite heavy and need a stable object as support. Use reel wire bound round to hold them to candlesticks, furniture, pillars or screens.

Special occasions

Candlelight and lamplight make a beautiful setting for church services in December.

Make certain that candles and lamps are positioned safely, and that plant material is placed well away from the flames of a candle or the heat of a lamp. Remember that short candles soon burn down. A garland or an arrangement of flowers at the base, or hung in an Oasis parcel half way down, can adorn a tall candelabrum. One or more candles can also be incorporated into a flower arrangement.

When a large block of Oasis is used for the mechanics it will support a candle. Mark the size of the candle by pushing it a little way in, then completely remove a round plug of Oasis of the same size, using a small knife. Replace with the candle. Then arrange the plant material around

AVERAGE RESOURCES *A candelabrum can be garlanded for Christmas; other furnishings are not hidden. Arranged by Jean Taylor and photographed by D. Rendell in St Wilfrid's Church, Mobberley.*

LIMITED RESOURCES *A candle arranged with long-lasting houseplant leaves and fruit by Hugh Mather. Photographer H. Leadbetter. Suitable for a city church with a scarcity of evergreens, but other leaves could be substituted.*

it, avoiding the placement of many stems near the candle so that the Oasis remains intact.

Small metal candleholders are available for pushing into Oasis or a roll of stiff ½-inch mesh wire netting, the diameter of the candle, can be used as a holder with one end pushed firmly into the Oasis.

Candlesticks of all sizes can be incorporated into arrangements of plant material at their bases, or flowers and leaves can be placed in candlecups on the top of candlesticks and these should be very safe. Inexpensive glass shields can be bought to place over candles if a draught is likely.

Oil lamps can be borrowed and look attractive in country churches placed on a cross-cut of wood with evergreens at the side. Sometimes oil lamps can be borrowed for a short while from members of the congregation.

LIMITED RESOURCES *A simple arrangement of holly and cedar
with artificial Christmas roses which could be fresh flowers if available.
The arrangement by Margaret Davies is kept well away from the lamp.
Photographer D. Rendell. By courtesy of The Flower Arranger.*

FESTIVALS AND SAINT DAYS

Christmas, December 25

This date was agreed, it seems, in the fourth century AD as the day for
celebrating the birthday of Christ, one of the two most important
festivals of the Christian year, the other being Easter. There are many
ancient legends concerning Christmas festivities and decorations.

The Romans celebrated the pagan Saturnalia near to this date with
good food, wine, singing and charades. Temples and homes were
decorated with coloured lamps and evergreens and part of the ceremony involved raising an evergreen bough. In the fourth century, when
the Romans adopted Christianity, there were great processions to
church on Christmas morning, to persuade people to replace pagan
associations by Christian observances.

The Norsemen also held pagan celebrations in honour of the sun on

261

the shortest day of the year which is also near this date. There was feasting and large log fires; shrines were decorated with holly, ivy and bay. Even the Druids decorated temples with mistletoe, considered sacred at this time.

For centuries evergreens have been symbols of life, when other plants are dormant. Candles are an ancient symbol of heat and light and in more recent times, symbols of Jesus and of truth to Christians.

An old German legend of the beginning of the Christmas fir tree is concerned with St Boniface, who went to Germany to preach about Jesus in the eighth century. He met a tribe worshipping a pagan god by sacrificing a young boy beneath an oak tree. The boy was rescued by Boniface who felled the oak tree leaving behind a tiny fir tree that had been growing between the roots. He told the tribe that from then on the fir tree should be a holy emblem, 'It is the wood of peace for your homes are built of it. It is the sign of eternal life because its leaves are ever green. It points to Heaven and shall henceforth be called the tree of the Christ Child.' Martin Luther is said to have first put candles on a tree, to remind people of the stars that shone over Bethlehem on the night of Christ's birth. Small electric lights are used now for safety reasons.

Nativity plays are a custom which came from Italy and St Francis of Assisi is said to have originated them with actors and live animals. Songs were composed by the actors to sing during the plays, using the peoples' own language instead of Latin, and singing then continued in the streets and is said to have been the origin of carol singing outside houses today. Most primary schools now have a nativity play which brings the Christmas story to children so vividly, in the same way as the Crib arranged in churches, with figures representing Mary, Joseph, the baby, angels, shepherds and wise men.

Ideas for Christmas decorations

Figurines

A crib can be arranged by the children with a vase of small flowers, evergreens or a tiny tree. Larger statues and figurines of Mary, if available, can be featured elsewhere in the church and decorated with flowers and foliage.

Trees

Trees can be used in larger churches. They can be cut or can be rooted conifers or bays borrowed from a garden centre or members of the congregation. An 'avenue' could be most effective in a cathedral. They

GOOD RESOURCES *A nativity scene in Wells Cathedral arranged by members of the South West Area of NAFAS. Photographer D. Rendell. This design could be made on a smaller scale.*

can be decorated in a number of ways such as with wired cones, small fruits or glass baubles. Gold baubles used alone can be effective in some churches. To soften the bare stem of a bay tree, flowers and foliage could be arranged at the foot in front of the plant pot, or at the base of the stem, in Oasis. It is important that the church is not over-decorated to the point where other beautiful permanent fixtures are hidden or movement is restricted. A writer in *The Spectator* of 1712 said that his church was so full of greenery that the middle aisle had been turned into a shady walk, and that the pews resembled so many arbours on either side of it. He added that the pulpit was so clustered with ivy, holly and rosemary that one worshipper commented that the congregation heard 'the word out of a bush, like Moses'.

Country churches
Driftwood, evergreens and frosted seedheads and cones look lovely in the country. Spray the seedheads and cones with clear varnish and sprinkle on a little glitter powder immediately (over a box to catch the surplus).

Carols
A group of skilled flower arrangers could interpret carols in various parts of the church, with a small card displaying the title of each.

Welsh traditional oranges
Three short 'legs' of strong branches are pushed into the bottom of each orange and a fat white candle with sprigs of evergreens is stuck into the top. The orange represents the world, the three legs the trinity, the evergreens eternity, and the candle the light of the world. A mass of these set on steps can look effective when the candles are lit.

A stand for a large decoration
For a large church a stand with three or more tiered shelves can be constructed to hold pots of poinsettias or other plants with tins or parcels of Oasis in front for evergreens. It need not be expensive and can be used for flowers during the summer or autumn. The stand is easily concealed by the plant material, especially when it is painted dark green.

Hanging arrangements
1. *Balls of evergreens* can be made of moss or of Oasis covered in wire netting. To make a moss ball, bind a handful of florists' moss into a spherical shape using reel-wire bound round about ten times to keep the shape. Before adding any plant material push through a long, doubled

LIMITED RESOURCES *Evergreens arranged in a Victorian church for Christmas by Stockton Heath Flower Club in All Saints Parish Church, Daresbury.*

stub wire. Turn the ends outwards and back into the moss. A long ribbon, nylon fishing line or wire can be used for hanging the completed ball from the top loop of stub wire. Push in sprigs of woody-stemmed evergreens such as box, to cover the moss. Clip for a formal shape but leave different lengths for an informal look. Flowers or small fruits can be added.

An evergreen ball

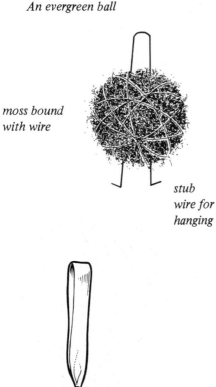

*moss bound
with wire*

*stub
wire for
hanging*

*wired ribbon
used for
hanging*

*turn up
ends*

*Add
sprigs of
greenery*

2. *Hoops of evergreens* can be made on a base of basketry cane, strong pliable wire or lampshade rings. The shape can either be spherical or a half sphere, like a crown. A similar style of decoration was made of bent twigs centuries ago and called a Kissing Bough or Bunch. It was decorated with candles and apples and mistletoe hung from the centre.

Bind long-lasting small-leaved evergreens on to the frame using reel wire. Gutta-percha (florists' tape) or bias binding can be used first to conceal the frame. Apples, cones or baubles and ribbons can be hung from it.

The year ends

And so the year ends for the church flower arranger, happy in the knowledge that the church has been made more beautiful through the bounty of nature and that people have been reminded of the wonder of the natural world created by God. Worship will have been inspired by the life and colour of the flowers and leaves, and those that have arranged them with patience and care will have made a significant contribution to the beauty of the church and the meaning of the services.

ACKNOWLEDGEMENTS

I thank the many people who contributed to the illustrations by arranging flowers so beautifully; those who generously lent photographs and provided ideas; Brenda Hall for her diligence in reading the proofs; Dorothy Cooke and Alice Kneebone for details of floral carpets, Anne Boase for her daffodil tree and Mary Tyler for a hassock of flowers; Richard Mulkern of Mowbrays and Canon William Purcell for their patience and kindness, and Douglas Rendell for many of the excellent photographs.